What People Are Saying
About A.J. Juliani and
Learning By Choice

"As educators, we all want to do our best for the kids we serve each day. As adults, we value having choices very much; however, how often do we allow our students to have choice in their educational journey? Juliani explores this notion of choice in an in-depth study of how giving students such opportunities can lead to higher levels of achievement and quality of their overall academic experience. His "10 ways" will not only transform your classroom but also change the way you feel about teaching; they're a must have for every classroom teacher!"

-Erin Klein, MACUL Michigan Teacher of the Year, ASCD Emerging Leader

"When it comes to student choice in the classroom, A.J. Juliani is both passionate and authoritative. His practical, step-by-step instructions take the often nebulous concept of choice and turn it into something actionable and manageable for classroom teachers."

-Angela Watson, Author of Unshakeable , Founder of The Cornerstone for Teachers

"Drawing from his experience as both a classroom teacher and an educational leader, A.J. Juliani provides deep insights and practical steps in how to infuse our classrooms with choice. The result is a clear, concise, and actionable book that will transform the way teachers approach differentiation."

-John Spencer, Teacher, Author, and Educational Speaker

Learning By Choice

10 Ways Choice and Differentiation Create
an Engaged Learning Experience for Every Student

by A.J. Juliani

Copyright © 2014 by **A.J. Juliani**

Press Learn

Ambler, PA 19002
www.presslearn.com

Publisher's Note: To order bulk copies please fill out the contact form at learningbychoice.com. To have A.J. speak at your organization, school, or company, please contact him at ajjuliani@gmail.com.

Book Layout © 2014 BookDesignTemplates.com

Learning By Choice: 10 Ways Choice and Differentiation Create an Engaged Learning Experience for Every Student/ A.J. Juliani -- 1st ed.
ISBN 978-1-5115685-9-3

To My Students
Don't Let Anyone Take Your Learning Away From You.

"Life is like a bicycle. To keep your balance, you have to keep moving."

—ALBERT EINSTEIN

CONTENTS

ON RESEARCH

There seems to be a notion in education that everything needs to be backed up by research. I too, as a teacher (and a parent), want to know that the instructional strategies I'm using in the classroom are best practices supported by studies, research, and experience.

Yet, I've also seen research change over time. I've seen us flip flop on what is best for students in the classroom. I've also seen a world changing so fast that sometimes it is difficult for research to keep up with the reality we see in our classrooms.

This book is not heavy on research. That does not mean I am against using research, or that there is no research to support the role of choice in student learning. Instead, I've sought to write a book that is filled with practical, step-by-step advice on HOW to bring choice into your classroom and create a student-centered experience regardless of what subject you teach or the age of your students.

If you are looking for a resource that will help you navigate choice, differentiation, and student engagement—then this book is for you!

If you are looking for research and theory to back up this type of teaching and learning, then I've got great news for you: I've listed over 40 books, studies, and research to support student-choice on my website, including:

- William Glasser's books: *Choice Theory* and *Choice Theory in the Classroom*
- Daniel Pink's books: *Drive* and *A Whole New Mind*
- Twenty different studies on choice and inquiry-based learning
- *Flow: The Psychology of Optimal Experience* by Mihaly Csikszentmihalyi

Throughout this book I add pieces of research to support suggested strategies and practices; but the real purpose of *Learning by Choice* is to give you ten different ways to bring choice into your classroom, and give you strategies to build a student-centered learning experience.

More information, resources, and research can be found at ajjuliani.com/research.

Thanks for reading!

LET YOUR STUDENTS CHOOSE

In 1915 Albert Einstein sent a letter to his son, Albert. Einstein was living with his second wife, and had not seen either of his two sons for quite some time. It was in 1915 that Einstein had finalized his theory of general relativity, and this letter to his son hints at that monumental achievement.

What I find fascinating about this letter is Einstein's thoughts on learning that he shares with his 11 year old son. I know that quotes from Einstein are thrown around online, and in presentations by educators across the globe…but this particular letter gets to the root of what matters in learning. In typical Einstein fashion, he writes it with such clarity and confidence, that not much else needs to be said:

> *What I have achieved through such a lot of strenuous work shall not only be there for strangers but especially for my own boys. These days I have completed one of the most beautiful works of my life, when you are bigger, I will tell you about it.*
>
> *I am very pleased that you find joy with the piano. This and carpentry are in my opinion for your age the best pursuits,*

EINSTEIN REFERS TO HIS WORK AS
STRENUOUS + BEAUTIFUL

Though laboreous at times, Einstein found pleasure in his work. ← Invested, Intrinsically motivated *better even than school. Because those are things which fit a young person such as you very well.*

Mainly play the things on the piano which please you, even if the teacher does not assign those. That is the way to learn the most, that when you are doing something with such enjoyment that you don't notice that the time passes. *I am sometimes so wrapped up in my work that I forget about the noon meal.* [1]

Einstein's message is this: Learn what you are interested in, and it won't "feel" like the learning we often partake in school.

What I find fascinating is how Einstein shares these sentiments after working eight years to prepare his theory of general relativity to be ready to share with the world. For Einstein, doing the work and learning, were tangled together. And, if it was work worth doing…something that he was interested in and challenged by, then it was worth working on for eight years.

DOING THE WORK + learning = A Fascinating Pursuit WORTH DOING

Choice and Flow in Learning

According to Mihaly Csikszentmihalyi, author of *Flow: The Psychology of Optimal Experience*, we are motivated to learn by two different reasons:

We either do some things for what we call extrinsic reasons. Namely, you work for forty hours a week so you can get a paycheck at the end. And you don't really like the job much but you want the paycheck to do things with that you will enjoy. So that's extrinsic because the reward comes after the activity from the outside.

Now, flow is a type of intrinsic motivation, that is, there you do what you're doing primarily because you like what you're doing. If you learn only for external, extrinsic reasons, you will

---

[1] Albert Einstein on the secret to learning:
http://www.farnamstreetblog.com/2015/02/albert-einstein-learning/

> *probably forget it as soon as you are no longer forced to remember what you want to do. Nor will you be motivated to learn for its own sake. Whereas <u>if you are intrinsically motivated, you're going to keep learning as you move up and so you are in this lifelong learning mode, which would be the ideal.</u>[2]*

In Einstein's example we can see hints at a state of flow when he is learning. He is enjoying the work so much that he forgets his lunch! This is the type of learning he wants for his son, Albert. And it is the type of learning that most teachers want for their students, and most parents want for their children.

How Does This Apply to Our Students

The problem in our schools is that <u>most learning is done for extrinsic</u> reasons. Students rarely have any choice in what they learn, how they learn, or how they are measured. We typically tell students what they have to read or learn, then lead them through teacher created activities, and finally test them traditionally on what they understand. There is no chance of falling into such a deep state of learning that they would forget their lunch!

[margin note: We tell students what to learn w/o considering how they learn.]

[margin note: Test Scores, P. approval, GPA, College Acceptance, Sports]

When I look back on my best learning experiences, most of them came outside the realm of traditional schooling, when I was able to choose what I wanted to learn. The result? I was invested in the outcome of my learning process because the experience was centered around the types of learning I do best. They were all student-centered learning experiences, and I was the student.

There are many people calling for school reform, and they have many different types of agendas and plans on the table. But I believe the key is for schools to change in one single fundamental way: **We need to let students choose as much of their learning path as possible.**

---

[2] http://www.edutopia.org/mihaly-csikszentmihalyi-motivating-people-learn

That's why I wrote this book.

This book identifies ten ways that any teacher can transform their classroom into a student-centered experience. Each chapter provides actionable steps for students to take charge of their learning path and be engaged and motivated by choice.

We will focus on real, doable ways to let students choose their learning path in any school and how you as the teacher can foster this experience in your classroom:

- Choice in what students learn through content selection.
- Choice in how students learn through various forms of instruction and activities in the classroom.
- Choice in how students demonstrate their understanding and academic abilities through a variety of assessment formats.
- Choice through differentiation and how a teacher can reach every student on his/her level.
- Choice in communication between students, student-to-teacher, and connection home.
- Choice in what types of technology students use and how they choose to present their learning.

All of this can happen in any school. You don't need to rip up the curriculum, you just need to think about it differently. This is the type of conversation we should be having in education because it is change that can happen and has happened already in many classrooms. So, let's start with a conversation and see what path it leads you down.

Your students will thank you.

CHAPTER ONE

Inspiring & motivating students by choice over what they learn.

CHOICE IN WHAT WE LEARN

I spent a lot of time as a teacher figuring out new ways to inspire and motivate my students. Sometimes it worked, but often I would fail to reach all of them. Then one day I gave my students choice. Not a "limited choice" assignment where they could pick one topic out of a box of topics…but REAL choice. You know what happened? Students were inspired and motivated to learn by themselves…and by each other. And they did a much better job at inspiring than I ever could. Choice gives students the ability to go above and beyond our curricular limitations…and allows them to innovate in ways we cannot predict.

That choice came in the form of the 20% Project (like Google) in my classroom.

Students could learn whatever they wanted to learn in my class…with no real limitations, for 20% of our class time. It was extremely difficult for some students, and for others it was very natural. However, the real magic happened when the students began exploring and learning about their "choices" during class time.

As a teacher I noticed some ways that choice impacted the learning process. Normally, we tell students what they are going to learn, then give them resources and materials to learn (sometimes created by us, sometimes created by others), then check for understanding, and provide feedback and help as needed.

This project was different because:

a) Students picked their learning topic and end goal

b) Students pre-defined what they would consider a successful learning outcome

c) In most cases I knew nothing about the topic they chose (i.e. I'm an English teacher and they chose to rebuild a car engine)

I was no longer the person with the most knowledge on the subject in the room, so I had to act fast and help in other ways. Pointing them in the direction of strong research and mentoring opportunities. Giving feedback on their blogging and documenting. Helping in the learning process (I was learning as well); and, I gave them a push towards some type of making/creating/building aspect in their project.

The Impact of Student Choice on Learning

20% of Classtime

There were five specific ways student choice of content impacted the learning going on in my classroom:

1. Choice Improves Student Buy-In

In the beginning of the project it was a challenge to get every student to actually choose a topic. Some wanted me to just give them a worksheet and tell them what they needed to do. However, once we got past this obstacle…the student's investment in their learning was already there. Students cared about what they were doing because they CHOSE what they were doing. If they complained about their topic, I would let them switch to a new one so the buy-in would always remain the same.

2. Choice Puts the Responsibility Back in the Students' Hands

At the same time, the students knew that I was not the "expert" on their chosen topic. One particular student choose to learn sign-language for their project. I didn't know sign-language so my responsibility as a teacher changed. Students could no longer come to me expecting an answer, but had to come to me expecting help in finding the answer. I was still the "lead learner" in my class, but I was learning alongside my students and not doing it for them. The learning responsibility was firmly on their shoulders.

3. Choice Allows for Flexibility

If you've ever done a "passion project" or wrote your own story, song—then you know that things change. The idea we initially start out with gets reworked and twisted into something completely new. Because I did not give requirements and deadlines with what they needed to complete, this project allowed for complete flexibility. Choice drove the students' actions and gave some room for lots of little (and sometimes big) changes along the way.

4. Choice Embraces Current and New Passions

To be honest, I didn't expect so many students to have no idea what they were interested or passionate about. However, this project allowed students to find new passions and new interests—as well as embrace their current passions. This is important because they did not need to start with base knowledge, but they also could start with base knowledge. That meant for many students they were just beginning to learn about this topic, and for others it was something they had been doing for many years. Choice put students on very different learning continuums during the project, but as we saw with the final presentations this did nothing to limit the overall learning.

5. Choice Leads to Growth

Ultimately, choice consistently led to growth in the classroom. Because of the above factors, choice became a way for students to create their own learning path, and assess how much they had learned. Almost every student came out of this project saying they had not only learned something new, but also been excited to grow through the process.

It was not always easy for my students (or for me as the teacher), but choice brought out the best in all of us as learners.

How to Bring Content Choice into Your Class: Go Beyond the Textbook

There are certain subjects where content is fixed to the curriculum. In most math courses you need to follow certain pathways to reach an understanding. In Biology the content is specific and you need to cover all of it...by the end of the year.

However, I've heard many teachers reference how they would like to move away from the "inch deep and mile wide" approach to curriculum. That is, they would rather teach depth of a subject than a wide breadth of information at the surface level. If your content is specific, give your students choice to go deeper into a specific area of that content and become an "expert."

If your curriculum is more skill-based like a Language Arts class, the content can be ever changing. Students can master the same skills by reading various different pieces of content. They can understand grammar rules by more than just filling in worksheets. In classes and subjects where "skills" are the main goal (like many elementary classrooms) giving student choice in content empowers the students to be engaged with material that is both relevant and meaningful to them.

A Step-by-Step Guide to Choice of Content in the Classroom

In order to successfully allow for choice of content in your classroom, follow these 7 steps (and modify as you see fit):

1. **Survey your Class:** What are your students interested in? What are their passions? What do they do for fun? Find out what makes each student tick, and what they'll want to learn more about.

2. **Fit the Choice to your Curriculum:** Do you have curricular constraints that you can't break? If so, try and fit the choice to your content area. Have students go deeper into a specific topic they enjoyed or were interested in a previous unit. Are their offshoots to work you've already done in class? Use various content to hit specific skills like reading, writing, listening, and speaking. Make it work for your students and your class.

3. **Create a Structure:** What times of the class/day or week are you going to give students the opportunity to learn what they want to learn? Make sure to keep a specific structure in place so students know when to expect this and when to be prepared. It also helps to try it in short bursts before delving into a marking period long project.

Create a System of Teach into Routines

4. **Start Small:** If I had to go back and do it all over again I would have started smaller. I would have given my students an opportunity to learn what they wanted to learn during 1-2 classes and present on their learning. Then I would have gone into a bigger project or unit where they could choose and have larger goals for what they would learn and do/create/make.

5. **Journal and Reflect:** As students begin to learn through their content make sure they journal on the learning process. What are they learning? What is interesting? What ideas do they have? Reflect on what the process is like and why they are motivated to keep learning.

6. **Make Something:** If all students do is learn, it can be tough to assess what they actually understand. One of the first

changes I made to my project is to make sure students created something to present to their peers after the project was complete. This idea of a final product also helped to centralize what they were learning, and give them an end goal for their work. As a teacher it helped me assess what types of learning the student did and where they could continue at a later point.

7. **Presentation:** After choosing a topic, researching, reading, watching, sharing, journaling, and making...the students need to present on their learning experience. Keep it short and simple. What did you learn? Why did you choose this topic/subject/area? What did you make? Let's see it! What went well and what would you change? That's it.

Remember, the goal of giving students choice in the content they learn is two-fold:

First, it increases engagement and self-motivation because they choose the topic. As I said to my students: only boring people are bored with this project!

Second, it allows students to learn important skills (and connects to state standards) that they'll need in your subject area and beyond; including research, presentation, and writing skills.

[handwritten margin note: Goals of Student Choice]

Start small and see what amazing things your students will accomplish!

Sample Project: A Standards-Based Choice Activity

Grade Level: 5-9

Subject Area: Writing (can be used in writing across the curriculum)

Purpose: Allow students to choose their learning topic, document their learning, and create a visual presentation to display their understanding.

Standards:

CCSS.ELA-LITERACY.WHST.6-8.2.A

Introduce a topic clearly, previewing what is to follow; organize ideas, concepts, and information into broader categories as appropriate to achieving purpose; include formatting (e.g., headings), graphics (e.g., charts, tables), and multimedia when useful to aiding comprehension.

CCSS.ELA-LITERACY.WHST.6-8.5

With some guidance and support from peers and adults, develop and strengthen writing as needed by planning, revising, editing, rewriting, or trying a new approach, focusing on how well purpose and audience have been addressed.

CCSS.ELA-LITERACY.WHST.6-8.6

Use technology, including the Internet, to produce and publish writing and present the relationships between information and ideas clearly and efficiently.

CCSS.ELA-LITERACY.WHST.6-8.7

Conduct short research projects to answer a question (including a self-generated question), drawing on several sources and generating additional related, focused questions that allow for multiple avenues of exploration.

Time: 180 minutes

Structure/Timeline:

1. Introduce the project to students as a way for them to learn what they are interested about or something they've always wanted to learn. Handout a project overview, goal setting sheet, and requirements (15 mins).

2. Have students fill out an "interest final four" - where they put their top four interests/passions against each other and choose a final winner to work on for the project (10 mins).

3. Have students answer three questions about their topic of interest (10 mins):

        a. What do you want to learn about this topic?

        b. Why does it interest you so much?

        c. How are you going to display what you have learned?

4. Time to research and document (60 mins):

        a. Have students research their topic using the internet, school library, and other online resources.

        b. Students should document what resources they have read/watched; and, what did they learn about their topic from that resource (use a double-entry journal).

        c. Students can document their learning in a notebook or online via blogging platform.

        d. Repeat steps A-C.

5. Share with a small group (20 mins):

        a. In groups, students can share what they have learned about their topic, where they've learned it from, and what else they want to learn before creating a presentation.

        b. Keep this structured to 2 mins of sharing, then 2 mins of feedback from the group. Short and to the point.

6. Final Research and Learning (30 mins):

        a. Go back and repeat earlier steps for learning with renewed focus on areas of interest after feedback from small group.

7. Presentation Creation (30 mins):

        a. Choose a presentation tool (can be multimedia or live display).

        b. Create a presentation with the following:

            i. Chosen Topic

            ii. Why you chose the topic

            iii. What resources you used

        iv.   What you learned about your topic along the way

        v.   Three takeaways to share from the learning

        vi.   What you would do different

        vii.   How others in class can get started learning about this topic

    c.   Practice the presentation

8.   Presentation (20 mins):

    a.   For time purposes either have students upload presentations online so they can watch regardless of class time, or create a gallery walk.

    b.   For gallery walk, have half of the class present for first 10 minutes and have students walk to topics that interest them.

    c.   Second half of class presents last 10 minutes.

9.   Final Reflection

.

Get more resources at learningbychoice.com.

CHAPTER TWO

CHOICE IN HOW WE LEARN

Take a moment and think about your favorite learning experience ever. What did you enjoy about it? Why did you get so much out of this experience compared to the thousands of other learning experiences you've had over the years?

Chances are you had a great teacher, a safe environment for learning, and something special that put this experience over the top.

As teachers, we want every student to have their best learning experience with us in our classrooms, yet our problem is that we often try to find the "something special" that will be the same for all of our students.

That's probably not going to happen.

Students (just like teachers and anyone else) learn differently. Some enjoy group work; others prefer to work alone. Some understand better through auditory learning, while others understand better through visual learning. The list of learning differences in students goes on and on.

As humans we each have specific sets of circumstances that allow us to learn best. This set of circumstances changes over time, and although it is fluid, a teacher does not have much control over what is going to allow a student to learn best that day.

Unless we give choice.

One of the basic tenets of differentiated instruction is that it allows a teacher to reach many students at different levels of understanding. By differentiating what we teach, and how we teach it, we are able to reach the entire classroom instead of the small group of students who are going to follow along with direct instruction.

Let's take this a step further and understand one important belief about instruction: **We are no longer the gatekeepers of knowledge. But, we are experts at how to learn.**

The gatekeeper method has teachers in the front of the classroom, or lecture hall, or computer screen, talking about what they know...and explaining how they came to that understanding.

Often we tweak the gatekeeper method by "spicing up" the lesson with technology or other fun activities. But, if the teacher (or textbook) is still the one holding all of the knowledge, it won't matter what types of activities you do, students will not feel they own the learning.

This is a key understanding because as a teacher we have the ability to teach the same skill one hundred different ways. Yet we often choose to teach the skill in one way. Maybe two ways. And if we are truly on top of our game – three ways.

When we differentiate, we build the choices into our instruction, and conversely the learning process. *That's a lot of work for the teacher.* It can be a lot of planning when we differentiate instruction. But what is our main goal for any learning activity?

Most would say our goal should be to have students demonstrate understanding of the concept/skill covered in the learning activity. I'd argue that *for any learning activity our goal should be engagement.*

Why engagement? Because student engagement predicts success better than any other metric in the classroom.

Engagement vs. Compliance

We know the best learning experiences happen when the learner's attitude, attention, and commitment to the process is at an all-time high. This combination is what Phil Schlechty calls "Engagement" in his fantastic levels:

Engagement (High Attention and High Commitment)

Strategic Compliance (Learn at High Levels But Do Not Retain)

Ritual Compliance (Learn at Low Levels and Do Not Retain)

Retreatism (Do Not Participate in Learning)

Rebellion (Develop Negative Attitudes Towards Learning)[3]

The issue with engagement is that many of us were taught that a classroom should look like the "strategic compliance" level. This is the "well-managed" classroom that many teachers strive to replicate on a daily basis, and the type of classroom that is often praised in classroom observations by administrators around the world.

---

[3] Schlechty Center on Engagement:
http://www.schlechtycenter.org/system/tool_attachment/4046/original/sc_pdf_engagement.pdf?1272415798

When you first walk into a classroom that may be loud, with kids all over the room, using different learning tools, some in partners, some in groups, and some alone, your first thought may not be engagement.

If you're not sure what engagement looks like, begin asking these questions:

1. What type of attitude does the student have towards the learning activity? What is the evidence?
2. What level of attention does the student have towards the learning activity? What is the evidence?
3. What level of commitment does the student have towards the learning activity? What is the evidence?

When you ask these three questions, as a teacher or administrator, the answers will lead you to an understanding of student engagement, compliance, or withdrawal.

How Choice Impacts Student Engagement and Instruction

In the first chapter we looked at ways to learn the same skill through a student-choice of content. In this chapter we are flipping that a bit. The reality of most schools is that certain content must be taught. Our goal is to figure out how to teach the same content through a student-choice of instructional experiences.

They key to this approach is getting all students engaged. That means all students must have high attention and high commitment.

One of the best and most manageable ways to do this is through in-class stations.

As a teacher, I used the station-model a lot, and I really believe it has the power to keep students engaged, moving, and working through different types of content.

(handwritten margin note: Reflection Questions)

However, when I asked my students about stations (especially at the high school level) I sometimes received feedback that they didn't like them. Why?

Well, many students said that they only liked a few of the stations and some of the other stations were boring to them. The stations they liked and the stations they thought were boring varied widely depending on the student and class.

I had my "Aha!" moment about stations during a fall football practice. As a coach you want to make sure the players are not only engaged but also focusing on skills that pertain to their position and role on the team. During the station part of our practice, the quarterback and receivers went to one station, the lineman to another station, and the running backs to a different station.

I thought, *why can't I do this in class?*

The difference would be allowing students to choose which stations they wanted to participate in, and giving them an opportunity to go deep with the content based on their preferred instructional activity.

When I brought this idea back into the classroom, my students were excited. They now had the power to choose, and from that choice came a level of ownership previously missing in station activities.

The Pick-Your-Station Activity

Here's an example of what a "pick-your-station" activity might look like:

First, you take the content/unit that is built into the curriculum. In this case let's use "photosynthesis" as our example.

Next, as a teacher you have to decide what instructional resources and methods you are going to use to deliver this content.

Instructional Resources and Methods Options:
1. Direct instruction (full class)
2. Direct instruction (small group)
3. Direct instruction (conference)
4. Read material (textbook)
5. Read material (articles)
6. Listen to material (podcast or audio)
7. View material (possibly flip the lesson with a video)
8. Listen/View/Read material (presentation with audio)
9. Photosynthesis online simulation

Traditionally, we'll choose one or two of these methods and create a lesson plan or activity based on what we believe is the best way to teach this topic/content.

Sometimes, as discussed earlier, we'll take four or five of these methods and create a station activity.

Here, you can pick five or six activities and let your students choose two or three that truly pique their interest.

It is important to note that there must be an assessment of some type that you are working towards. In this case, we'll use a photosynthesis lab as our final project-based assessment.

In order for students to successfully complete the lab and analyze the results, they'll have to understand:

a) What photosynthesis is and why it is important.
b) What the process looks like.
c) Key terms and vocabulary for the content.
d) How this connects to other units in science that you've covered.

The "Pick-Your-Station" activity provides this information in a variety of formats and experiences. As students choose the station, you'll get a better grasp on what types of activities work for them, and which ones they find engaging.

Throughout the stations, students should be recording what they are learning, and what they understand through a guided set of notes.

The end result is that all students should be prepared to successfully complete the photosynthesis lab activity.

Previously, in a traditional classroom setting, students may have not been engaged through a presentation, or did not connect to the instructional delivery method. Here, they have the choice to go with what works best for them as a learner.

A Step-by-Step Guide for Your Classroom: Pick-Your-Station

1. Identify a unit/concept or skill and what you want students to know/do/make in order to demonstrate their understanding/proficiency.
2. Create or choose an assessment that allows students to demonstrate mastery.
3. List various instructional methods, resources, and strategies to prepare students for the assessment.
4. Choose four-six instructional methods to turn into station activities. Each station activity should be a similar length in time and cover common material. Here is where you can add different types of technology or hands on experiences to the learning process.
5. Create a workflow at each station for the students to follow. Have notes and formative checks as part of the station design process. Allow for reflection at each station when planning how long students will complete the activity.
6. Introduce the different stations to students and describe what the goals of the activity are (as well as the assessment this is leading up to).
7. Let students pick two-three stations based on their interests.

8. Start the timer and keep rotations from station-to-station even. As the teacher, a few of the stations might need more guidance than others. Make sure you aren't just "managing" this activity, but instead truly acting as a guide and expert learner at various stations.

9. Once the station rotations are complete, put students into small groups to "jigsaw" the reflection. Bring students from different stations together to reflect on their learning experience and share.

10. Listen to reflections and check the formative pieces for each station to see if every student is prepared for the assessment. If not, feel free to go through one more station together as a class or talk about any topics/concepts they did not understand during the activity.

11. Give the assessment (see Chapter 3 for more on this!)

As you can see, the process may take a little more time on the front end from the teacher, but you'll know that students are prepared for an assessment by going through this activity.

When I began using technology in the classroom, these activities also turned into online experiences that could be done at any time. My ultimate goal as a teacher was to see my students succeeding and demonstrating understanding of concepts and skills at a high level. The simple act of "giving students choice" changed how my students viewed our assessments, and how they prepared for assessments.

For more resources on this topic, please visit learningbychoice.com/chap2.

CHAPTER THREE

CHOICE IN ASSESSMENT

My first full year of teaching was as an eighth grade Language Arts teacher. It was my dream job at the time. I loved the energy of middle school students, and I was still taller than most of them.

What made my job even better than expected was our teaching schedule. Because our MS teams had two language arts teachers, I taught three eighty-five minute blocks, instead of five forty minute blocks. Although this schedule meant more time teaching, there were fewer students per class and for my course load. It helped in grading especially (think of how long it takes to grade 130 papers versus 65 papers).

An added benefit that I did not see when I started the school year was how much extra time it gave me to understand and get to know my students. When you spend eighty minutes a day for 180 days you really get to know someone. I think of the connections elementary teachers can make with their students and know this bond is even stronger.

Midway through the school year one of my students asked me if I'd share some of my own writing with them. I actually couldn't believe I had not done this yet. I had shared some examples of papers that I crafted, but although these were original, they weren't connected to the type of learning that I often did outside of school.

I told them I'd read something I wrote the next day. Oddly, although we did a lot of fun activities, it seemed like my students were more excited than they ever had been before. .

That night I took out a memoir-type piece I had recently wrote about a friend passing away and how it changed my outlook on life. I wondered if this was "too heavy" for my 8th grade students, and then remembered that we all deal with loss and hopefully this could show how I grew since this tough time.

As I read aloud the memoir, "Three Bands on My Wrist", to my students they sat and listened quietly. There was no technology involved. There was no particular instructional strategy being employed. It was just me, my words, and their attention. After I finished they wanted to write their own memoirs and we began that same   class period.

I can honestly say that some of their writing that week was the most inspired I have seen in all my years teaching. And it was their choice. The next year I moved up to the High School English department, and two years later I was teaching tenth grade English to many of the exact same students I had in eighth grade.

When they came into class, I already knew each student I knew their backgrounds, family situations, interests, and learning tendencies. I was a bit more challenging as a tenth grade teacher and that ruffled some feathers early on, but after that we were able to do some high-level types of activities because relationships were already built.

However, I did have one problem. Although I knew them personally, I wasn't able to see how much they had grown as writers over the past year. I had kept a few papers from that eighth grade year, but not enough for every student. When I asked the ninth grade teachers if they had saved any of their papers, the answer was "no." There was no student work to look at.

This was another light bulb moment for me as a teacher. Because we usually start fresh with students we have never taught before, we tend to want to make our own judgments on their abilities from the first few assignments and assessments. It's from those first glances that we base our opinions and pedagogical strategies on for our students.

Yet, with this group I had taught them a year and a half ago. I knew them and what they could do, but still wasn't able to see how much they had grown in the past year. That is when we made the decision to start digital portfolios. I highly recommend doing this, not only for teachers, but for entire departments and schools. It adds true choice to the assessment process. Here's why.

What Can Students Do? The Portfolio Journey

We always want to know what our students understand and are able to do/apply. The problem is that a multiple choice assessment rarely provides that information. But they are used because they are easy to grade, easy to distribute, and easy to re-use year after year with various updates. It is why many standardized assessments are multiple-choice and why the SAT and ACT use this model for most of their questions.

Not only do multiple choice assessments not provide the best information about students' abilities, what's even worse is that the idea of "data-driven" instruction is based on these various multiple-choice assessments and what they say about our students' abilities.

What kind of learning do these assessments promote?

1. Regurgitation and memorizing facts from study guides or stories
2. An "only one right answer" mentality

3. The rewarding of smart guessing and "playing the game"
4. The idea that answers have to already be in your head

The list could go on. As a former teacher who gave multiple-choice tests, and an SAT Tutor for years who taught students how to take these tests, I'm embarrassed to say I also once tied rigorous and tough multiple-choice questions to deep learning.

But I saw firsthand when I had that group of eighth grade students again in tenth grade, what kind of information I can get from different forms of assessments. I was able to see how they did on standardized and district level assessments, but unless their scores were off the charts (high or low) it didn't give me much information on what kind of learner they were or what kind of work they could produce. What I can see by looking at student work is much different. A student portfolio shows me the following:

1. What the assignment/activity/assessment was and how the student approached it.
2. What kinds of personal experiences and biases they brought towards the assignment.
3. How well they demonstrated an understanding of the content.
4. How well they demonstrated their skill ability.
5. Usually some kind of reflection or meta cognitive piece on what they did.
6. If they improved or not with the next piece in the portfolio.

It's not only what every teacher wants to see from their former students, but it also makes it much easier to assess the growth of a student over the course of a semester or full year class versus how much a final test or culminating project would show.

Portfolios helped me to visually see where my students were struggling and where they were exceeding my expectations. Portfolios also allowed for student choice in the assessment process, which as we know leads to student engagement and ownership of their learning.

Choice in Demonstrating Ability and Understanding

Because we love multiple-choice so much, let's take a quick quiz:

A student is trying to demonstrate their understanding on the rise and fall of Napoleon. In order to show what they know about this historic time period and the reasons behind Napoleon's rise and fall, they can be assessed through which activity (circle all that apply):

a) Writing a five-paragraph essay on the rise and fall of Napoleon

b) Creating an infographic on the rise and fall of Napoleon

c) Creating a political cartoon and rationale on the rise and fall of Napoleon

d) Creating a five-minute mini-documentary on the rise and fall of Napoleon

e) Creating a fictional serial-like podcast of interviews with key players in Napoleon's life

f) All of the above

Don't you just love the "all of the above" option? In any one of the above options you could assess a student's understanding of the topic/situation and their ability to demonstrate the appropriate skill. What's different about this scenario, is the choice provided to students allows them to engage in the material and claim some ownership over the assessment activity.

A Step-by-Step Process to Creating Choice-Based Assessments

If you are not familiar with the "Understanding by Design" framework, I highly recommend checking out *Understanding by Design* by Grant Wiggins and Jay McTighe. In UbD (as it is commonly referred) you use the backwards design process to create units.

For our purposes this is extremely important. We want to create the assessment first, and then backwards design the unit so that the content and activities students are doing matches the skills and standards covered on the assessment(s).

Step One is choosing your unit (this is most likely decided by your current curriculum).

Step Two is choosing the skills you want your students to master and the applicable standards for the content and skills you are covering (hopefully this is also somewhat covered by your current curriculum).

For example, let's say the unit is all about "historical figures" in your state/area. You have a set curriculum and text to read (often an informational text such as a textbook). This current example can be for fifth grade. Jump onto the standards **website** and search for applicable standards for fifth grade "Reading: Informational Text" to find this:

CCSS.ELA-LITERACY.RI.5.1
Quote accurately from a text when explaining what the text says explicitly and when drawing inferences from the text.
CCSS.ELA-LITERACY.RI.5.2
Determine two or more main ideas of a text and explain how they are supported by key details; summarize the text.

CCSS.ELA-LITERACY.RI.5.3

Explain the relationships or interactions between two or more individuals, events, ideas, or concepts in a historical, scientific, or technical text based on specific information in the text.

Step Three is now putting the pieces together for various assessments. The assessment must focus on similar content (historical figures), similar skills and standards (see the above three we will hit on), and have a similar rubric for grading.

Let's talk about the rubric for a moment. Here's where many teachers get stuck, because creating a grading rubric takes a lot of time. And who has that much time!?

Lucky for all of us there are some very easy and efficient ways to create standards-based rubrics online. My favorite tool is essaytagger.com/commoncore.

It took me less than five minutes to create this sample rubric based on our example standards:

Example Common Core Rubric (LBC)
Common Core-aligned rubric (5th Grade)
shared by Created by A.J. Juliani
www.EssayTagger.com/rubric?code=

	Below 5th (weakest)	Beginning	Emerging	Proficient	Above 5th (strongest)
Quote Text in Explanations (¶) paragraph-level Reading: Informational Text: RI.5.1					
Quote Text in Inferences sentence-level Reading: Informational Text: RI.5.1					
Determine Main Ideas (¶) paragraph-level Reading: Informational Text: RI.5.2					
Key Detail Support whole document Reading: Informational Text: RI.5.2					
Summarize Text whole document Reading: Informational Text: RI.5.2					
Explain Relationships or Interactions (¶) paragraph-level Reading: Informational Text: RI.5.3					

What's nice about EssayTagger is the ability to personalize and change all of the categories above in the top row. The categories down the side are straight from the standards and skills we pulled for this unit.

Ask yourself after creating the rubric, "Can this work for various types of assessments for this unit?" If the answer is "Yes", then you've got a rubric to work with. If the answer is still "No" you'll either have to create a new rubric or revisit Step #2 for some clarity.

Step Four is allowing your students to choose their preferred assessment or create their own assessment. As we discussed in Chapter 2 with the "pick-your-station" activity, choice empowers students and engages them in the material.

I used to have a bank of various assessment types that my students could look through and choose the assessment that best fit their personality, interests, and learning styles. However, over time more and more students started to use the first option on that list: Make your own assessment.

Some of the assessment ideas that came from students include:
- "I want to make a Saturday Night Live parody skit around this topic, and poke fun at the way it was handled in a historical sense."
- "I want to conduct an in-depth interview with the author, where my friend will play the role of the author, and we'll get into a heated argument."
- "I want to create a flip-book style comic to show the character's story arc."

This list could go on. Students are much more creative in their assessment ideas than I ever could be!

Step Five is conferencing with students on their plan. You'll want to make sure students understand the following:

- What the end-goal is for this assessment
- How they are being assessed (look at the rubric together)
- What the expectations are for their work
- What a time-line looks like for their assessment
- An action plan of how they are going to get it finished

This is one of the most important pieces of allowing choice in assessment. A traditional assessment dictates all of the terms listed above. You know when the test date is, what type of content is going to be on the test, how much each question is worth, when the study guide needs to be completed etc. But here, the short conference serves as a guiding plan for completing the choice-based assessment, and demonstrating a high-level of understanding.

My students always felt better after this mini-conference because the goals, outcomes, and steps were clearly laid out in front of them, as well as how they would be ultimately assessed on their project.

Step Six is digitizing the project and sharing it with the class and in their portfolio. Regardless of what assessment type students choose, they need to create a digital record of this assessment to put in their online portfolio. This is easy to do if the work was done on a digital device, but if it was not, you'll need to take pictures (or video recordings) to upload to the portfolio.

Teachers ask me all the time what they should use for student digital portfolios. I'd first recommend using a platform that your school is already using (Google Apps for Education, Microsoft 365, or Apple options).

By starting out with a simple Google Drive (or SkyDrive) folder, you can eventually give the students a choice down the road of what platform they want to create their digital portfolio so they can share it with the world. Here is where students will make their own website: using Wordpress.com, Weebly.com, Wix.com, Squarespace.com, and many more options.

Step Seven is grading the assessment (teacher grade and student grade). A big piece of this type of assessment is to have students grade themselves using the rubric. They were fully aware (from the earlier conference) what was expected and how their work demonstrates understanding. The act of reflecting and grading themselves makes this all the more transparent.

After students grade themselves, I would look at the rubric and their assessment to see if I had different thoughts on what was demonstrated. Interestingly, most of my students were incredibly honest throughout this process and were harder on themselves than I might have been when grading them.

If the student's grade and my grade were completely off base, then I would have another short conference to talk about expectations and outcomes for this assessment so we could get on the same page.

Step Eight is actually assessing the portfolio itself. At the end of the unit, marking period, semester, or year, it's important to assess the overall work of the student through their portfolio. Art teachers have been doing this for years, and more and more colleges are requesting to see real student work as part of the admission process.

To make a real word connection, think of your students' digital portfolios as the first steps in their academic resume, but also in crafting their personal brand and professional identity.

The choices they make in what they create/make/do for assessments, will directly impact the choices they make in their career and life path. If they do not document this journey, then it will be hard to reflect on why they made choices and what they have learned along the way.

For more resources and information on this topic, go to learningbychoice.com/chap3.

CHAPTER FOUR

CHOICE IN DIFFERENTIATION

When Khan Academy burst onto the scene my initial reaction was to laugh. What was so special about it? Khan Academy touted its site as an online learning platform with vides on almost every subject. Khan Academy let teachers "flip their instruction" by presenting the lesson/lecture at home through video, and working on what would have been homework in school with the teacher.

The more and more I thought about Khan Academy and the idea of "flipping your classroom" the more I became frustrated with the general public's perception of teaching and learning.

If the media and public believed that watching videos at home the night before school was a solution to all of our educational problems, then what was the point of teaching at all!

I was annoyed, a bit angry, and generally confused at how this platform could be seen as such a savior.

In the midst of my frustration, I went to look at what others were saying about Khan Academy and the idea of "flipping the classroom" with video. I was an English teacher at the time, and it didn't make sense to me. We had always sent the content home in the form of reading, and done the work in class in the form of conversations, formative assessments, Socratic seminars, and analysis.

Investigating the Khan Academy learning method led me to another "aha" moment. I realized that I didn't really know what teaching looked like in other subjects besides my own. Like many teachers, I was so wrapped up in my own content area that I forgot that students went to six other classes a day in our high school.

Two years after this epiphany I left the classroom for a new role as a K-12 Technology Staff Developer. Now I was tasked with helping to integrate technology into the classroom and run our 1:1 laptop initiative at the high school. My new job was something I always wanted to do. I loved working with my colleagues, and I was especially passionate about the transformative role technology can play in the learning process.

That year I grew more as a teacher in than any other time in my career for one reason: **I watched other teachers teach.**

I helped teachers plan, watched them teach, talked about their subject areas, or their grade levels (in elementary school), and reflected on what worked well and what could be improved. Although my focus was on technology, the real discussions happened around instructional strategies, pedagogy, and best/next practices.

After a year, I better understood what the entire scope of an educational experience looked like. I had previously held assumptions about subjects like science, math, and social studies from my own middle and high school experiences as a student. Sure, I had cross-curricular conversations over the years with my colleagues in these areas, but never before had I seen what it took to plan and execute a lesson, activity, or assessment in their subject areas.

Without a doubt I was most blown away by the math teachers in our school. Students came into their classrooms with a preconceived notion about whether they were good or bad at math. Most of the math skills built upon each other, so if students had previously struggled and "just got by" the year before, they would come in behind, possibly fall farther behind, and struggle again throughout the school year.

It was a snowball effect–and the snowball got bigger and bigger each year.

Math classes were also where I saw some of the biggest need to differentiate. Students were on various levels of understanding for all kinds of concepts. There was no possible way you could "teach to the middle" and actually help the students who were struggling, or challenge the students who had already mastered the concept/skill. Teaching "to the middle" left two-thirds of the class with ineffective instruction, and the teachers I worked with knew this struggle all too well.

I was planning with a third-year math teacher who caught me off guard when she said:

"I'm constantly checking to see if they understand what we are doing, but when 80% of the class gets it that means five of my students are falling behind when we move forward. Not only that, but another five to ten students understand the material so well, they could possibly teach most of it to themselves at the pace we are going…"

I thought: *there has to be a better way.*

That's when I went back to the idea of Khan Academy. Instructional video lessons were a possible solution to this problem that was most likely repeated in schools across the country and world. The videos could serve as remediation, or to push some students farther ahead who worked at a quicker pace with that concept.

In theory, the idea was great.

But, like many good ideas, in practice it didn't work too well. Students had to want to watch the video–just like any homework–and students had to understand the instruction in the video for it to work. The problem was that sometimes it was not high quality instruction, and there were no teachers to answer questions while the video was playing.

When we discussed the idea of "flipping the classroom" in our math classes, we wanted to focus on how it could help teachers differentiate, instead of just send home instruction for homework.

What came out of this discussion and planning was an amazingly simple and effective way to differentiate and provide some structured choice in the learning process. It was both simple for the students to understand, and effective in how students could move from a low-level of understanding to a high-level of understanding. And it was an engagement boost!

The difficult piece was designing the lessons and activities in order for this type of differentiated flipped model to work successfully. Luckily, we had some amazing teachers who worked incredibly hard to develop this model.

Let's break it down.

The Three-Tiered Flipped Model for Differentiation

As we walk through these ten steps to "flip" your instruction and set up a working model of differentiation in your class, keep in mind a few things.

First, realize that this can work in any subject area. In order for it to work successfully, a teacher must come up with clear objectives on what students need to know, and how they will demonstrate that knowledge. You'll also have to be able to teach the main concept through video, and students will need a way to access that video at home.

Second, don't spend too much time thinking about the resources you use to make the video. I'll share some that work really well in the final part of this chapter, but often teachers get stuck in the technical side of things instead of just making it, and getting better with production over time.

Third, make sure you use this strategy to find out what your students know and what they are missing–then get them to a place where they can demonstrate that understanding. Differentiation may sound difficult, but really it is providing various pathways for students to achieve the same level of success. When you pre-assess students, the goal is not to see "who did the homework," but instead how your instruction can meet students where they are at in their current level of understanding.

A Step-by-Step Guide: Choice in Differentiation

Here are ten steps (some longer than others) to get this model working with your class:

1. Teachers identify a particular concept or skill to focus their instruction (often dictated by your curriculum).
2. Teachers create a short video screencast (using Screen-cast-o-matic.com) walking students through the concept, explaining the reasoning and steps, providing examples of the skill in action.
3. Teachers edit and upload the video to Youtube or Vimeo.
4. Students watch the video the night/day before class and take notes or answer some quick comprehension questions.
5. When students arrive at class the following day, the teacher hands out (or gives digitally) a short five question pre-assessment based on the video and instruction from the night before.

6. Students answer the questions to the best of their abilities and then score a partner's assessment (or self-score their own).
   a. Students end up in three tiers based on the pre-assessment score.
      i. Score a 0-1 and you are in Tier A.
      ii. Score a 2-3 and you are in Tier B.
      iii. Score a 4-5 and you are in Tier C.
7. The goal for all students is to end up in Tier C by the end of class.
8. First third of class:
   a. Tier A sits down and re-watches the video from the night before with a teacher created handout with new questions.
   b. The teacher gets Tier B into groups (or partners) to work on refining some of the skills and concepts together. They can use the video as a guide, and call on the teacher to help during their group work.
   c. Tier C is given a higher-level application challenge.
9. Second third of class:
   a. Teacher heads over to Tier A after video is complete to answer any questions they might have on the concept and give the entire group some questions to answer. Then they answer questions individually. They move onto Tier B.
   b. Tier B takes another short formative assessment (individually) to show their understanding after the group work on the concept. Those that score a 4-5 move onto Tier C.

    c.   Tier C continues to work on the challenge or completes it and begins to help new students coming into their group.

10. Last third of class:

    a.   Tier B students work in partners or groups and take the next formative assessment when they are ready. Teacher floats between Tier B and Tier C helping and challenging as needed.

    b.   Tier C students finish challenge and work to create a challenge for the following class (or next year's class).

    c.   Tier B students are helped by classmates and teacher to move to Tier C before the end of the class.

Let's recap the goals achieved through these ten steps:

First, you start with some type of work at home or in the beginning of class. Then you assess quickly each student's base knowledge of that concept. The pre-assessment separates your class into three tiers of understanding. The goal is to move students through tiers and provide different levels of support, with all students landing at the final tier for a challenge activity by the end of class.

The key to making this successful is to embed choices into the activities during class. Allow students to pick partners and groups. Give students multiple types of questions to answer and activities to complete. Give the second tier options on how they are assessed before moving to the final tier. Provide the final tier with options and choice to challenge their understanding and move past the application to a higher-level of thinking.

I would recommend starting with a concept or skill that some students typically master more quickly than others. In this case, you will have already experienced the frustration of having students at all different levels of understanding and know that there has to be a better way to instruct the entire class.

Start small with a short video, and quick activities at each of the levels. That way, when you move into bigger units of study, students will be familiar with the process and expectations. It's amazing to watch the negative "snowball" effect of students falling behind stop immediately. In this model there is no "falling too far behind" because students are all expected to reach a certain level of mastery by the end of the class. Choice and formative feedback are the fuel that gets them there!

To access more information and resources on this topic, go to learninbychoice.com/chap4.

CHAPTER FIVE

CHOICE IN COMMUNICATION (AND RELATIONSHIPS)

In 1936 Dale Carnegie wrote a book called *How to Win Friends and Influence People*. It went on to sell over 30 million copies. It still sells today and is probably one of the best books on how to improve your social skills.

In his little book, there are so many insightful quotes and lessons on how to actually "get along" with people and have some influence. As leaders and teachers, this is a great book to learn from. We are constantly striving to have a positive impact and influence on teachers and students…yet we often put that "skill" on the back burner.

Instead, we focus on debating the Common Core, talking about the next big thing in Educational Technology, and looking at how many different ways we can "reform" education.

Maybe some things do need to change our focus has to stay on positively impacting the lives of students in our school.

The Real Influence We Have on Students

In the Journal of Student Engagement (2012) Lauren Liberante writes:

The teacher–student relationship is one of the most powerful elements within the learning environment. A major factor affecting students' development, school engagement and academic motivation, teacher–student relationships form the basis of the social context in which learning takes place (Hughes & Chen, 2011; Roorda et al.,).

Teacher–student interactions are not only influenced by a number of aspects including gender, but in turn also influence a student's academic outcomes and behavior. Supportive and positive relationships between teachers and students ultimately promote a "sense of school belonging" and encourage students to "participate cooperatively in classroom activities" (Hughes & Chen, 2011, p.278).

Liberante's research makes the case that the relationships in our education system may prove to be the most effective way to improve student engagement. All of us that teach and work with children understand the importance of relationships. We know that spending time helping a student one-on-one does more than a small group setting. Yet, we often forget how much influence we can have on a student's learning.

Daniel Coyle, author of *The Talent Code*, recently looked at a new study on feedback from teachers. This study showed that **one simple phrase could boost student effort by 40%.** I was shocked when I read this, but in the back of my mind I was already guessing what the phrase would be…and I was right on the money. See for yourself:

A team of psychologists from Stanford, Yale, Columbia, and elsewhere recently set out to explore the question: What's the secret of great feedback?. They had middle-school teachers assign an essay-writing assignment to their students, after which students were given different types of teacher feedback. To their surprise, researchers discovered that there was one particular type of teacher feedback that improved student effort and performance so much that they deemed it "magical." Students who received this feedback chose to revise their paper far more often that students who did not (a 40 percent increase among white students; 320 percent boost among black students) and improved their performance significantly.[4]

What was the magical feedback? Just one phrase:

I'm giving you these comments because I have very high expectations and I know that you can reach them.

That's it. Just 19 words. But they're powerful because they are not really feedback. They're a signal that creates something more powerful: a sense of belonging and connection. ~~will~~ feed back, always provide

Yep. I knew it had to do with expectations and potential. As a high school English teacher, my students always responded when learning was presented as a challenge. Specifically, a challenge that I "expected" they would reach. This phrase, and the effect of 40% more effort, is so important. Are we teaching pre-service teachers about simple things like this? Are we focusing professional development on boosting student-teacher relationships?

Back to Dale Carnegie's Work

Carnegie's book has many lessons for teachers and leaders: Simple reminders (like the one above) that can lead to deeper conversations, better relationships, and a stronger influence on students' learning. Let's look at ten phrases from *How to Win Friends and Influence People* that bring us back to the basics of teaching and learning.

---

[4] http://thetalentcode.com/2013/12/13/the-simple-phrase-that-increases-effort-40/

"If you want to be enthusiastic, act enthusiastic."

Ferris Bueller's teacher: not enthusiastic. Randy Pausch from *The Last Lecture*: enthusiastic! Which would you rather learn from? A teacher and leader's enthusiasm carries over to their students. It carries over to the learning. I always wondered why we focused so much on "content" during pre-service teacher training. The teacher should already be passionate about what they are teaching. If you aren't…then maybe you shouldn't be teaching. If you want your students to be pumped about learning, you need to first look at yourself and see what kind of enthusiasm you are bringing to the classroom.

"Any fool can criticize, condemn, and complain but it takes character and self-control to be understanding and forgiving."

Guess what? Kids are going to let you down. They are going to miss assignments, forget to read, fail your test, maybe even cheat. But don't adults let us down too? Every great relationship must have forgiveness and understanding attached to it…otherwise it is more of an "agreement" or "partnership"…not an actual relationship. Hold students accountable for their mistakes. Then forgive them and empower them.

"The royal road to a man's heart is to talk to him about the things he treasures most." (and) "You can make more friends in two months by becoming interested in other people than you can in two years by trying to get other people interested in you."

Talk to your students, or your teachers (if you are an administrator), and find out what they are interested in and passionate about. Spend time crafting ways for them to explore their passions and interests. In doing so, you'll let them think of you as someone they can talk to and learn from about "what they want to learn". This is the essence of inquiry in our schools: it works because they care.

"There are four ways, and only four ways, in which we have contact with the world. We are evaluated and classified by these four contacts: what we do, how we look, what we say, and how we say it."

Do you come to work every day as a professional? Make no mistake about it: improving relationships is not about dressing like students and "getting down to their level". It's about being professional every day. Dressing the part, looking the part, and acting the part. I remember those substitute teachers that kids used to harass when I was in school. There biggest flaw: not looking the part. It may sound silly to focus on this, but I believe it is incredibly important. We trust doctors that are in scrubs. We trust lawyers that are in suits. And we trust teachers that are professional each and every day.

"I am very fond of strawberries and cream, but I have found that for some strange reason, fish prefer worms. So when I went fishing, I didn't think about what I wanted. I thought about what they wanted. I didn't bait the hook with strawberries and cream. Rather, I dangled a worm or grasshopper in front of the fish."

Do you bait your students with strawberries and cream? Do you focus on what interests you when you teach? Or do you understand that our learners want something else. Find out what engages your students (you can do this from conversations) and use it! Maybe it is something to do with technology, maybe it is a connection to something in pop culture…but whatever it is, use it to boost the learning experience. Great teachers find new ways every year of delivering content that would otherwise be stale.

"People rarely succeed unless they have fun in what they are doing."

So simple. Yet, we often forget this in the world of standardization. Make sure you teach above the test. My good friend Steve Mogg and I taught 11th grade English. At the end of the year we had finished our fourth book with some type of mystery in it. We decided to put our students through a made up CSI case for a week. We devised an entire back story, and each day the students had to find more and more clues. The classes battled against each other to solve the mystery. It was a lot of fun. It was a lot of fun and they learned more that week than any other week during the school year!

"Develop success from failures. Discouragement and failure are two of the surest stepping stones to success."

I firmly believe that "successful failures" are they key to growth in school and life. I see this time and time again in and out of school. Do you allow time for you students and/or teachers to fail? Do you provide opportunities for them to learn from those failures? If not, you are missing out on one of the biggest influences on learning.

"Inaction breeds doubt and fear. Action breeds confidence and courage. If you want to conquer fear, do not sit home and think about it. Go out and get busy."

What are you doing right now to positively influence the learners and people in your life? Are you waiting for something to change? Are you waiting for the right moment? Stop waiting.

Do something right now. You may fail. You may succeed. Either way you will learn and set a great example. Let's use the research at our fingertips to inspire our own teaching and leading. We know what drives great learning experiences: relationships. It is your choice as a teacher and leader as to how you build those relationships!

But Communication Is Always Changing...

One of the hard things about building relationships and communicating with students is choosing how to communicate. Face-to-face is usually a great way to build rapport and have meaningful conversations, but we don't always get a chance to have one-on-one conversations during class. Our students are also living in a digital world. They communicate heavily through technology...yet we often struggle with how to build relationships in a digital way.

The best thing you can do is give students choice in how they communicate with one another in and out of your class, and in how they communicate with you. There is no reason to dictate what the communication channels are going to be when those channels are always changing, evolving, and revolutionizing the way we communicate and collaborate with one another.

Fifteen years ago (when I was in high school) cell phones were just breaking into mainstream use. My parents let me get one because I was driving and they thought it would be a good idea to have in case of an emergency.

I didn't use it to text anyone. In fact, I thought (along with many of the people reading this book) that texting was so silly when I first heard about it. Why would I want to take the time to "text" someone a message when I could just call them instead???

Flash forward five years from my first cell phone and all I did was text. Facebook had recently come into our lives and now I would get in touch with friends by texting, instant messaging online, or writing on their Facebook wall. I rarely called someone unless it was my mom.

Five years later and everything had changed once more. The iPhone. Twitter. Group chats. And today my wife Snapchats me photos of our kids, I stay in touch with friends over Instagram, and share professionally on Google+. My siblings and I rarely text, but we do use Group messaging platforms like "What's App" over 500 times a day. Communication is on demand through a variety of platforms on my phone, in my watch, or embedded into my car, house, etc.

So, with all of this change...why do we limit how students communicate in our classrooms (and outside of our classrooms)?

It's time to reassess how students communicate with each other, how they communicate with their teachers, and how they collaborate on authentic work using digital (and not-so-digital) tools.

As the Dale Carnegie quote mentioned above, don't use strawberries and cream when a worm would work better. Take time to give students choice on what types of communication works for them, and then build on that to create great relationships and collaboration between students and teachers.

A Simple Guide to Choice in Communication and Collaboration

First, give out a survey to your students at the beginning of the school year or new semester. With younger students this survey can be done informally. The survey should include questions about what type of communicator they are as individuals and what communication tools they use the most in their everyday lives. Again, this will change depending on age and grade level.

Second, review the results as an entire class. Pull out trends and show where the high percentages are for a shared communication tool. For example, when I did this with my students a few years ago, "Twitter" was the top communication tool that students used on a daily basis. But...we did not immediately choose Twitter as our class communication tool.

Third, discuss as a class what communication tools they would like to use for each of the following purposes:

1. Teacher-to-class communication. Is this through a texting platform like Remind? Or a social network? Or maybe through a Learning Management System? Or just email...

2. Student-to-student communication. Set expectations of what this communication should look like. Again, what is the main platform that the class will use.

3. Student group work communication and collaboration. How will students best collaborate with each other in group situations? What platform or communication tool works best.

Fourth, create common communication and collaboration expectations and guidelines for students. Then allow choice to take over in the tools that they use. An example of guidelines would look like this:

Students will choose the best platform/tool to stay up to date on class assignments, updates, due dates, and schedule. If this communication platform/tool is not working properly they will let the teacher know immediately.

Students will choose the best platform/tool that work for them and their classmate when working together. This choice will be discussed in their first meeting time and will be used throughout the process. If this communication platform/tool is not working properly they will let their classmate know immediately.

These guidelines allow for choices to be made in communication tools and how students collaborate with one another. Which brings us to step #5.

Fifth, remember to iterate. I made the mistake of allowing my students to choose their communication and collaboration tools like it was the wild, wild, west. After three weeks it was complete chaos. Groups were fighting over what tool they wanted to use, and complaining about not receiving information that they needed.

When we decided to start using a Learning Management System (examples include: Schoology, Edmodo, Canvas, Blackboard, Moodle) as our hub for communication, it eased a lot of this in-fighting over communication. What I learned was my students wanted choice, but they also were fine with that choice being limited to a degree. With the LMS we had a hub that they could all access and rely on for information. That allowed other students to use secondary forms of communication to work and collaborate. Without a chosen "hub" we were a bit lost, and that is why iteration is so important. Not only does technology change, but people also change how they work.

The **sixth** and final step is the most important. Don't make all communication and collaboration digital. Give real face-to-face interaction the most time in your classes. Regardless of whether or not students live in a "digital world", they still enjoy the social aspect of learning together, and working with each other in real group situations.

Do not forget the influence that we (as teachers and leaders) have on our students. The same can be said for the influence students have on one another. A great classroom functions as a team. Have common goals, common language, and common expectations of each other. Communication is one piece that cannot be forgotten or put to the side, it is just as important to give choice in communication as it is for content, assessments, and activities.

Learn more about choice in communication and get free resources at learningbychoice.com.

CHAPTER SIX

CHOICE IN PACE AND ORDER

Bobby was an 11th gradê student in my English class, and he was angry.

"I don't understand this project, Mr. J. What are we being graded on and when is it due?"

I looked around at the class to see a handful of students just like Bobby. They weren't used to this. In their 11 years of school, the game had been simple. A teacher like me would tell them what they needed to know, give them some homework and class work to gauge their understanding, and then review and test them on whatever concept they should have "mastered" by now.

"There is no grade Bobby," I said. "I want you to learn whatever you want to learn, and share your experience with the class".

Bobby turned from my gaze towards his backpack and muttered, "This is stupid" under his breath. I could sense the tension in the room, but I wanted to make a simple point to my 11th grade honors students: School isn't a game to be played and learning doesn't always need to have points attached to it.

If you've been following my blog or read my book *Inquiry and Innovation in the Classroom,* you may recognize this scene from when I introduced the "20% Project" to my students for the first time a few years ago. I had many students like Bobby who were frustrated with the notion of learning for learning's sake, instead of for points. Yet, I don't blame Bobby or any of the students I had for thinking this way. They've been taught since a very young age that school is a game and if you follow the rules, it is easy to win.

I want to make this clear to teachers and parents right now: Teaching our kids to play the "game of school" will not help them later in life. Instead, it will teach them that learning is measured only extrinsically and failure is not an option.

This Isn't A Race

I recently read a piece by author and entrepreneur Oliver Emberton, "Life is a maze, not a marathon". In this post I continued to substitute the word "life" for "school" as I was reading and it opened my eyes to a simple question: What are we teaching our students about life, through the process of school? Here's what Emberton has to say:

Imagine if life were a marathon.

There's a start, a finish, and the faster you run, the further you go: The secret to winning a marathon is to knuckle down and keep going.

Most of us treat life like this, but reality isn't so two dimensional. Real life has no signs, and no straight lines. There's just a maze of infinite options:

Some paths, like some careers, take five times longer to get where you want. Some paths, like some relationships, are dead ends.[5]

Are we teaching students that life is a marathon, or a maze? If life is a marathon then maybe our current view on school works, but if life really is a maze (and Emberton makes a good case) then we have to agree on this: Working hard and following the rules is no longer good enough.

How to Shift Away From the Game of School

It's very easy to criticize something like the "game" of school. We've all played it (or resisted it and been labeled failures) on some level throughout our lives. We play similar games in certain jobs and industries as well. Yet, the reality of work right now, and the near future of work has completely changed what students will be doing once they leave our schools.

In Will Richardson and Rob Mancabelli's white paper, "Preparing Students for a New World of Work in the 21st Century", they make this argument:

Schools were built for a time when access to knowledge, information and teachers was scarce, restricted to what we could find in our local libraries and communities. But with the advent of the Web and our growing abundant access to all of those things, the form and function of schools is now in question as the needs of our students begin to shift in some dramatic, important ways.

They continue to make the case for five important shifts in the workforce: *The rise of self-employment, rapid job switching, the rise of the robots, works goes mobile, and the employee as their own*

[5] http://oliveremberton.com/2014/life-is-a-maze-not-a-marathon/

brand. Each of these shifts make our past education system more and more obsolete.

So, it's become clear that:

1. Life is not a marathon, and school should not be one either.

2. Work is shifting in ways we can't truly predict, and students will have to navigate new choices.

Moving away from the game of school has to start with parents and teachers. If we continue to set up the same learning patterns and experiences students will quickly realize the best way to succeed in the school setting is to "play the game". To move away from the game we have to make three shifts in the way we teach and parents need to support these shifts:

First, we need to give students choice in their learning experiences and support them when they fail.

I cannot stress this enough. The way we naturally learn is by experimenting, failing, and learning from our failures. Having only "one opportunity" to take an assessment is not a natural way to assess understanding or any sort of competency. Having only one "way" to assess is not natural. We learn differently. Let's respect that in the learning choices we give students.

Second, we need to teach students to treat challenges as opportunities.

This mindset is so important and must be modeled by the adults as well. There will be challenges. Learning is not always easy: in fact, it's usually difficult. But, if we treat challenges as new opportunities we'll also be preparing students to overcome those challenges once they leave our schools and go through the maze of life.

Third, we then can teach students how to make their own game…instead of playing in a pre-designed one.

Think of the really successful people in our world. Most of the time, they re-defined what success could be and what it could look like. Many of them did not "wait for their turn" or pay their dues. Sure, there was trial and tribulation and tough times. But they made choices to take a different path to success. They created their own game and changed the rules.

Giving Students Choice in the Game They Play

Our current system of schooling traditionally dictates the order of learning for our students and the pace at which they can learn and grow. We plan the entire learning path, we tell students how long the path will take, and we rarely give students a voice in how they get to the end of their path.

Then, all of a sudden, we want students to make a choice. A big choice. *What do you want to do with your life?*

After high school students have to choose what they are going to do. Are they going to college? Are they going to a trade school? Are they jumping into the work force? Are they going to start a business?

Students also get to choose how long it will take for them to accomplish each of these things. They get to pick the order. They can change the pace at any point in time.

As a teacher, it may be easy to throw our hands up in the air and say, "There is no possible way I can give students choice in the order of work that they do and the pace while still covering the curriculum and everything my school is asking me to do!"

And you would be right. And you would be wrong.

You are right in the sense that it seems impossible. But you'd be wrong, because there are ways we can give students choice in the pace and order of their learning, despite the restraints we have placed on us from all sides.

Here are six-steps that can take you from "hands up in the air" to "I can do this" as a teacher.

Step-by-Step Process for Choice in Pace and Order

1. Focus on the End Result (What Students Know, Understand, and are Able to Do) ∪ ßL

This is crucial to making any changes to instruction. As a teacher, you need to clearly understand the learning outcomes for any particular unit and/or lesson. What does understanding look like, you may ask? I always go back to a quote from the "Teaching for Understanding" project at Harvard:

> If a student "understands" a topic, she can not only reproduce knowledge, but also use it in unscripted ways. For example, a student in a history class might be able to describe the gist of the Declaration of Independence in her own words; role-play King George as he reacts to different parts of it; or write out parts of an imagined debate among the authors as they hammer out the statement. These are called "performances of understanding" because they give students the opportunity to demonstrate that they understand information, can expand upon it, and apply it in new ways.[6]

In the first three chapters we showed how students can demonstrate their understanding and abilities in a variety of unscripted ways. When teachers and students both have a clear view on what the learning outcome will be, there is flexibility in how to get there.

---

[6] http://www.pz.gse.harvard.edu/teaching_for_understanding.php

2. Plan a Flexible Path

The traditional path to understanding in a unit of study looks something like this: Student reads content, teacher discusses the content and reiterates key points, student discusses content with peers and often does activities associated with that content that covers specific skills. At the end of the unit the student demonstrates mastery of that content (and skills) by completing a summative assessment.

Planning a flexible path, gives the student choice in how they navigate away from this traditional approach. It also provides multiple opportunities to differentiate by content, process, product, and environment. As Carol Ann Tomlinson says in her book, *The Differentiated Classroom: Responding to the Needs of All Learners,* 'A great coach never achieves greatness for his team or himself by working to make all his players alike.'

Give students choice in how they get to an understanding they can demonstrate in unscripted ways. The path can be different and full of choices, as long as we are all headed to the same destination.

3. Self-Assessment Checkpoints

The best way for students to regulate their own pace and order of learning is to have self-assessment checkpoints throughout the unit. Checkpoints can be put in place while planning a flexible learning path, or they can be called out at any time by a teacher.

The key is to get students to truly self-assess themselves without any fear of judgment by peers or teachers. We know that self-assessment and reflection is one of the most powerful factors of learning. Give students multiple opportunities to assess their own work throughout the unit, instead of only at the end.

4. Allow for Mastery

Rick Wormeli, author of *Fair Isn't Always Equal*, has a view on "Redoing work" hit home for me on so many different levels:

> *If we do not allow students to redo work, we deny the growth mindset so vital to student maturation, and we are declaring to the student:*
>
> *-this assignment has no legitimate educational value*
>
> *-it's okay if you don't do this work*
>
> *-it's okay if you don't learn this content or skill*
>
> *None of these is acceptable to the highly accomplished, professional educator.*[7]

One of the quickest ways you can give students ownership of their learning, is to really focus on the learning as growth, not a fixed outcome. That can be started by allowing students to re-do work, and re-take assessments. Do you do that already?

5. Allow for a Change in Pace

In the book, *Finding Flow: The Psychology of Engagement With Everyday Life,* author Mihaly Csikszentmihalyi makes this comment:

> *If you are interested in something, you will focus on it, and if you focus attention on anything, it is likely that you will become interested in it. Many of the things we find interesting are not so by nature, but because we took the trouble of paying attention to them.*[8]

We have this balance as educators. Students still do not yet know what they will be interested in during their lifetime, but they also have

---

[7] https://www.adams12.org/files/learning_services/Wormeli_Response.pdf

[8] https://creativesystemsthinking.wordpress.com/2014/02/24/flow-the-psychology-of-optimal-experience/

current interests worth pursuing. Allowing for a change of pace gives students the flexibility to dive deep into a piece of new content they find interesting. Or take a longer amount of time working on a project where they've found a flow. It also gives students the choice to move quickly through tasks or activities that they might not like, but understand need to be completed in order to work on a project they are excited about.

6. Be Open to New Learning Avenues

Each of these steps opens up the possibility of learning different. The traditional path to learning does not necessarily work as well with non-traditional learners. Our students live in a world of constant distraction, on demand information, and multiple types of content. Choice in pace and order opens up not only flexible learning paths, but also completely new learning avenues that have not yet been explored.

To get more resources on choice in pace and order, visit learningbychoice.com.

CHAPTER SEVEN

CHOICE IN TECHNOLOGY

Why are you using technology? Or more importantly, how are you using technology to better the learning in your classroom and/or school? If you are like me, then you've had your fair share of technology screw ups. Projects that didn't make sense (but used the "tech" you wanted to bring in). Activities that were ruined by a crashing website or some technological problem. And of course you've probably dealt with the students, parents, and teachers that want to do things "the old way" because that is what they are comfortable doing...

In order to make sure you are using technology the right way, you must first *start with why*. If your students understand the "why" behind your technology use, then the class will have a purpose and technological glitches and issues can be worked through. If they don't understand the "why" then any small issue could turn into a major problem.

Here are 7 ways I've been using technology for a purpose in my classroom and as a staff developer in my school. I'm sure there are many other ways to use tech with purpose, but these are some of my favorites!

1. To Collaborate in Real Time

Remember when Google Docs broke onto the scene? It was magic. Students writing and sharing in real-time, able to see what the other students are doing and saying, while still working on your own part of the project or activity. Flash forward 7-8 years and now *real-time collaboration* is a must for most online software. This type of technology allows project-based learning to be monitored, documented, and done outside of the school hours.

At my school we have been using Microsoft OneNote (as well as the Google products) to collaborate in real time. Whether it is staff planning together, students working together, or a combination of both...this technology has so many learning purposes.

2. To Reflect and Share

I used to have my students journal in their marble notebooks. And during certain activities I still do (like Writer's Boot Camp). However, what's nice about having students journal online and share "in the cloud" is the ability for their classmates to see what they have to say.

This is why I suggest blogging throughout the year, and not just as a project. Make blogging a part of your student's life and you'll be able to see which topics, ideas, projects, and activities really impacted them. Sometimes it may not be what you thought...and sometimes their simple act of sharing will bring the class together in ways you never could have imagined.

3. Better Research

After I finished writing my Master's thesis on 'peace education in the 21st century' I talked with my mom about her writing process in graduate school. It sounded awful... She would have to go to the library, find a resource, read almost the entire resource, make copies of the pages she wanted to use, and literally cut it out and paste it on her typewritten document.

Technology has made research simple and more time efficient. I'm not talking about typing a question into Google, I'm specifically focused on searching journal databases like ERIC through places like Ebscohost. A nice search phrase will turn up hundreds of peer-reviewed results which can be sorted many different ways (such as by date or full-text article). Those articles that you choose can then be automatically scanned for your keywords, read the specific parts you want, and use what is applicable with a simple copy and paste and proper citation already set up and ready to go.

How often do we really teach students how to research in today's world? Or do we expect them to learn on their own like we did?

4. Write and Rewrite

Using tools such as Google Docs, the new Microsoft Word, or Draft students are able to write and edit on the fly. They can get feedback from peers and teachers and then choose whether or not to accept that feedback on their writing. This goes for presentation platforms as well (Google Slides, Prezi, and Microsoft 365 PowerPoint). Technology has changed the writing process in much the same way it has changed the research process.

The most important part of writing is the revising and editing. Yet, we often take it for granted. Instead let's use the technology to track what types of changes students have made, and if they are making the same mistakes in their writing over and over again. That way, the rewriting process can have a direct impact on how much they improve and change some of their writing habits over time.

5. Make Something (that matters)

This may be my favorite way to use technology with a purpose. Students now have the ability to make movies, songs, pieces of art, websites, apps, games etc–with technology. However, too often we ask students to make something that does not matter. We ask them to make a movie or poster or presentation that has no direct impact on the world around them.

Instead, let's challenge ourselves to start making technology matter. Make iMovies that can be uploaded to Youtube and have a purpose. Make games with a meaning. Make apps that matter. Yes, there is a time for fun and games. But if that is all we use technology for in school then we shouldn't be surprised when that is all students use technology for once they get out of school.

6. Keep a Digital Record

Digital portfolios are a must (as we looked at in Chapter 3). Not because colleges will want and need them in the future (which is happening sooner than you think). Not because it is a cool way to show off what you've done in class. Digital portfolios are a must because they show learning growth.

The best way to show how much a student has learned is through a digital portfolio. You can look back over time and what they've created, written, and done in school. And how that work has improved (and in what ways) throughout their schooling. When students know their work will be on display and recorded, they also take pride in what they do because it will last.

Ask yourself, are you making "digital fridge art" or something worth keeping?

7. Mastery Assessments

Think about the last time you gave an assessment. I'm sure you prepared students for it during class, gave them materials to study, and supported them during the assessment. However, there were definitely a few students who struggled on this assessment. What happens next? You can either give them a re-take, give them another similar assessment, or say that is their only chance.

If you gave them a digital assessment you'd be able to see exactly which questions they got wrong in comparison to the entire class. You could see how much time they spent on the question and if the answer they chose was way off base or close. You could tailor a new assessment based on just the problems/questions they got wrong and make sure they achieved mastery on those topics before moving forward.

There are many more ways to use technology with purpose, but these are a great place to start. The problem we often see with technology is teachers who believe it is something separate from their actual instruction. When we make technology *special* it does not reflect the real world where technology is an integral piece to work, relationships, and livelihood. In order to use technology as a transformative learning tool, we have to look at it from a different angle then we did 10 years ago.

Don't Put Limits on Something That is Always Changing

Technology is changing at an incredible rate right now. It's not progressing by 10% each year, but actually doubling exponentially in many different areas. The iPad was revolutionary five years ago and today sales are beginning to plummet. Wearable technology is beginning to take a place in the market. And by the time you read this, something else will have "revolutionized" education as we know it.

I've heard this question in various forms many different times: **How is technology going to save education?**

Radio and TV were going to save education, but we all know they didn't. They changed consumption from primarily reading or live viewing to listening and watching, but the prediction of televisions replacing teachers in the classroom has yet to come true. Computers and devices were going to save education. The internet was going to save education. In fact, it seems as though every time a new technology changes our way of life (radio, tv, computers, internet) we believe it is going to save education...

Let's stop thinking about technology as a cure or savior for education.

Instead let's realize that great learning experiences have always had similar patterns and pedagogical strategies...and technology can be a part of that experience sometimes.

Let's also stop thinking about "educational technology" as something that needs a massive amount of training.

Instead understand that teachers, students, and parents are all on different parts of the technology continuum and will need varied support depending on their experiences. It doesn't matter if you are a digital native, digital immigrant, or digital explorer much of how you use technology will have to be learned through using it, not through training (because much of what you are trained on will change soon thereafter).

Let's stop believing that new tools will revolutionize education.

Instead understand that new tools often substitute, sometimes augment, and very rarely redefine the learning experience (thank you, SAMR). It is how the teacher and students use these tools for learning that truly matters. And when technology is used to redefine a learning experience, the revolution is what the students make, create, and build with their tech, not in the many ways they can consume information.

What choice does to technology is bridge the gap between "digital natives" and "digital explorers" in the classroom. Students learn from students. Teachers learn from students. And students also learn a lot from teachers. Just because a student knows how to use an iPad to play games, watch Netflix, and listen to music...does not mean they know how to use it as a true creation tool. This is what we can learn from each other if choice plays a role in how we use technology.

A Step-by-Step Guide: Let Students Choose Their Technology

We've established the role of technology in education as something that has to have a direct learning purpose. We've also made it clear that technology is not going to "save education" but how we use it can transform learning experiences.

Here's what this section is not going to be: a debate on BYOD. This is not about bringing your own device to school. This is about allowing for choice in the classroom when technology is available for learning purposes (regardless of how it got there).

Technology can be used for almost every aspect of the learning experience:

- as an instructional tool
- as an assessment tool
- as a collaboration tool
- as a communication tool
- as a creation tool
- as a data tool
- as a writing tool

And the list could go on and on...

Step 1: As a teacher, you must first decide on the purpose of technology in the learning experience. Are you using it for an activity, an assessment, or something else? Why are you using technology? How will it transform the learning experience?

Step 2: Next, you'll have to decide if technology is going to substitute, augment, modify, or redefine the learning experience.

I recommend using the SAMR Model to decipher how you are using technology. SAMR is a model of tech integration designed by

Dr. Ruben R. Puentedura, Ph.D. that is simple, easy to gauge, and offers all educators something to strive for.

SAMR MODEL

Redefinition: Tech allows for the creation of new tasks, previously inconceivable

Modification: Tech allows for significant task redesign

Augmentation: Tech acts as a direct tool substitute, with functional improvement

Substitution: Tech acts as a direct tool substitute, with no functional change[9]

The goal of course is to get to the "**Redefinition**" level on the SAMR Model. However, sometimes you'll have to start with enhancement uses before reaching the transformative uses.

For example, using Google Docs to write an essay might be a necessary task your students have to complete. Google Docs auto-saving feature and cloud storage provides functional improvement over older Word processing software (this would be at the **Augmentation** level).

If your students use Google Docs to collaborate in real-time on the document in and out of class, then technology allows for significant task redesign from a traditional essay writing process (this would be the **Modification** level).

If your students then shared those documents with other peers around the world to get input and feedback on a position taken in the essay, we've now hit the **Redefinition** level where technology allows for a task that was previously inconceivable.

---

[9]http://www.hippasus.com/rrpweblog/archives/2014/12/12/SAMR_DevelopmentTeachingPractice.pdf

Step 3: Find out what technology students already know how to use and what they are currently using in their own lives. How does this experience and technical knowledge fit into the learning objectives and purpose for technology?

Step 4: Give students the choice to pick an appropriate technology for the task. For example, if they want to make a presentation, they can choose between PowerPoint, Prezi, Google Slides, HaikuDeck, or hundreds of other presentation tools out there online.

You might be asking, "But why can't they all use the same tool/platform so it is easier for me to grade and learn?"

I made that choice many times as a teacher. I forced my students to use a specific tool or platform because I knew how to use the tool and would be an expert in the classroom.

What changed my mind over time was a renewed focus on two things:
1. What was best for the students
2. What really matters with technology

What's best for the students is their ability to choose a platform/tool they either know how to use or one that they want to learn to use. This choice is significant (and we've gone over the same rationale in previous chapters) because it empowers the student's experience and gives them ownership in their learning.

What really matters with technology is not using the tool, but how to effectively and successfully use technology for a learning purpose.

That's why it's as important to know how to use Excel or Google Sheets...but instead understanding how to use "spreadsheet" software for a learning purpose.

The same goes for presentation tools, word document tools, and video editing tools. Learn how these programs, tools, and software functions...and you'll be able to re-learn a new tool for a transformative purpose, regardless of how much technology changes over the years. If you want to learn more on this topic (including some great resources and guides), go to learningbychoice.com/chap7.

CHAPTER EIGHT

CHOICE IN STORY AND PRESENTATION

"Science, by its own definition, doesn't give us meaning. It just provides us with facts . . . Our lives gain meaning only when we tell our story."—David Steindl-Rast

A few years ago I was lucky enough to teach the book, *Things Fall Apart* by Chinua Achebe, to my 10th grade English class. It's a great book…but that's not why I was lucky.

I had recently been to Africa two times and learned so much from the people there, and now I finally had a book that related to my experiences. Each day in class I had another story to tell, and when we missed a day of storytelling in class, my students eagerly asked me if I had any more stories, or if we were just going to have a regular class.

That comment opened my eyes to the power of stories in my own classroom. My students wanted to hear about my experiences because they connected to those stories. As we read through the book and discussed Okonkwo's (the main character) motivations and actions, there was a deeper understanding taking place.

Soon, we were all sharing stories that related to the book. Okonkwo had wanted to be a different man than his father was, and now his son wanted to be different than he was. Young men and women in my class spoke about the pressures they put on themselves to live up to their parents, or be different than their parents. We began to relate to the deeper conflicts in this book, because our stories connected with them as well.

I'm a big believer in project-based learning and inquiry-driven learning...but there is something special about story-driven learning. My students ended up scoring better on their quizzes and projects for *Things Fall Apart* than any other book I'd ever taught. From that moment on, I knew there had to be something to the power of story.

The Science Behind Storytelling

Humanity

Every night before my daughter goes to bed I tell her a story. Sometimes it is based on the day's events, and other times it is a story about when I was a child, but usually it is completely made up...and she loves it. She also vividly remembers the stories later on.

If I hit on a similar theme or topic in my bedtime story the next day, or next week, or even next month...she calls me on it. She lets me know that I talked about that before, or that this sounds like the other story I told her... She'll also relate our bedtime stories to real events that happen, and many of the same themes and topics that come up in our stories...come up in our lives.

This is not unique to my daughter, instead it is based in science and research. "A 2010 study in the Proceedings of the National Academy of Sciences showed an intimate connection between the brain activity of speakers and listeners in conversation, demonstrating how the brain of an engaged listener "syncs up" with a speaker. By engaging students with compelling stories that impart important material, teachers reach students both emotionally and biochemically, increasing the potential for rich learning experiences."

Sherrelle Walker – a teacher, administrator, and professor of 30 years – wrote about the science behind stories:

> *Scientists have long known that human beings are storytelling creatures. For centuries, we have told stories to transmit information, share histories, and teach important lessons. While stories often have a profound effect on us due to emotional content, recent research also shows that our brains are actually hard-wired to seek out a coherent narrative structure in the stories we hear and tell. This structure helps us absorb the information in a story, and connect it with our own experiences in the world.[10]*

So, if you are like me, maybe this is all starting to make sense. I know that I learn best through experience and stories. If I think back on some of my best learning experiences they were often either having to do with hearing a great story...or creating a new story. When I look at what articles I enjoy, they almost always teach me something through a story. That is the initial hook of many great learning experiences.

But yet, so often in our techno-focused world we fail to take the time to actually teach through stories. I'm guilty of this, you might be too. Technology is a great tool for learning, but guess what, storytelling might be a better tool.

Stories, Technology, and Innovation

Pamela Rutledge is a Professor and Director of the Media Psychology Research Center. In an article she wrote for Psychology Today, Rutledge says:

---

[10] http://www.scilearn.com/blog/using-stories-to-teach.php

> *Even with technology's increasingly sophisticated and jaw-dropping capabilities, the tools are becoming simultaneously more accessible and user-friendly. So much so, that the boundaries are blurring not just across technologies but also across the people who are creating, using, producing, augmenting, distributing, hacking, mashing, and every other '-ing' imaginable.*[11]

In spite of all the excitement, however, the human brain has been on a slower evolutionary trajectory than the technology. Our brains still respond to content by looking for the story to make sense out of the experience. No matter what the technology, the meaning starts in the brain.

The research has shown that stories fuel understanding of all types of learning objectives. If you want your students to…

- understand mathematical principles
- write better essays
- learn through inquiry
- apply scientific theories
- tackle real world issues
- innovate in the classroom

…then teach them with stories.

Leo Widrich, the co-founder of Buffer, wrote a fantastic article on the science behind storytelling. He explains that our brains can't help but function differently when we are being told a story:

> *When we are being told a story, things in our brain change dramatically. Not only are the language processing parts in our brain activated, but any other area in our brain that we would use when experiencing the events of the story are too. And yet, it gets better.*[12]

---

[11] http://www.psychologytoday.com/blog/positively-media/201101/the-psychological-power-storytelling

[12] http://lifehacker.com/5965703/the-science-of-storytelling-why-telling-a-story-is-the-most-powerful-way-to-activate-our-brains

When we tell stories to others that have really helped us shape our thinking and way of life, we can have the same effect on them too. The brains of the person telling a story and listening to it can synchronize, says Uri Hasson from Princeton:

> *When the woman spoke English, the volunteers understood her story, and their brains synchronized. When she had activity in her insula, an emotional brain region, the listeners did too. When her frontal cortex lit up, so did theirs. By simply telling a story, the woman could plant ideas, thoughts and emotions into the listeners' brains.*

Anything you've experienced, you can get others to experience the same. Or at least, get their brain areas that you've activated that way, active too.

What does this mean then for our teachers and students?

First, it means we should spend some time rethinking the "best practices" in instruction. Stories are often told in History and Language Arts classes, but are they used effectively? And are we ever thinking about teaching with stories in the STEM subjects? For example, John Spencer's book, *Wendell the World's Worst Wizard*, teaches "making" and "STEM" concepts through the story of a young wizard with no magical powers.

Second, I'd argue that one of the most innovative ways to teach may be to slow down, and tell a story. Figuring out what story to tell, and how it connects, is the job of any great teacher. If we want our students to change the world, they'll need some inspiration from the stories of those that have already changed the world.

Finally, books like Kendall Haven's *Story Proof,* is a must-read for anyone who is teaching anything. Haven's book explores more than 150 qualitative and quantitative research studies that discuss the effectiveness of stories and/or storytelling on learning. Let's use the research we have to improve how we teach.

Somehow I was never told to "teach with stories" when I was starting out as a teacher, even though that is one of the best ways in which I learn. However, "story-driven learning" may be one of the most underused and oldest methods of teaching and the most effective.

Choice in Telling Their Story

In almost every classroom, in every subject and grade level, we ask students to tell stories. Sometimes those stories are for language arts papers and essays. Often they are for a history report. However, in almost every subject we ask students to give or complete some type of presentation.

The presentation can be a daunting task for any student: Get up in front of the entire class and describe your learning. I've seen students break out in hives, faint, and cry many times during a class presentation. And I blame myself.

As a teacher, I want to see how my students can present an idea, event, or findings in a professional manner. Sadly, this usually ends up looking like a boring power point, filled with too many bullet points, too much text, and too few pictures. I sat through these types of presentations with my 8th grade students before realizing what was missing.

A Step-by-Step Guide to Choice in Presentations

I created a three step process to prepare my students for presentations that I still use today when I get ready for my own presentations.

First, make the expectations of the assignment clear, but allow the presenter to create their own "why" for the presentation. I'd generally recommend giving choice for the topic and assignment, but this isn't always the case. Usually, this is pre-built into our curriculum and the topic and assignment will have been created for the students. The presentation could be about the pyramids in Egypt, but I want to know why this is important. The students have to "choose their own why", which is basically how they are crafting meaning from this topic, and what they want to share with the audience. If the student has a "why" and is not just listing facts...we are on the road to a better presentation.

Second, I want them to focus on how they tell the story. In does not matter if you are presenting on a lab report in science or pythagorean theorem in math class...it's how you present the information that matters. When I first began focusing on the "story aspect" of presentations my students began to call me out during class when I was teaching with a particular type of story. They learned the eight different types of presentations well by the end of the year, but let's start with four that can be used at any grade level:

> ***The Hero's Journey:*** *Forced from the world they know, the character (which could be the student) has to move into an unknown place, go through a series of trials, before being helped by a guide (could be the internet or resource), find success, and then come back to their original place with knowledge that can help in multiple ways.*

> ***The Climb:*** *Much like a TV series, the journey to a final result is long and arduous with multiple trials happening along the way. As they fight for knowledge and understanding, they begin to appreciate the journey itself, before a final climatic moment happens and the problem is resolved.*

> ***Sparklines:*** *The most famous presentation style has the presenter sharing the ups and downs of the journey. Presenting a dark reality with an optimistic view on what could be...Martin*

> *Luther King Jr's "I Have A Dream" speech is a great example of this style.*
>
> ***The Action:*** *Start the presentation with the most interesting aspect of the work, and catch the listener's attention. Then circle back around to the beginning to show how you got to that place. Think of how CSI shows the crime, before going back and taking you through the story before the crime, and what happens to the final conclusion.[13]*

There are many different ways to tell a story in a presentation, and I would argue there is no "right way", but some work better for certain types of assignments. The benefit of this type of presentation style is what we talked about earlier in the chapter: Humans learn best through stories and experiences. By framing the presentation in a certain narrative structure, students create better connections with their audience, and also have the mindset of a story-teller instead of someone presenting a collection of facts and findings.

Third, allow them to choose how they present the story to their audience. The rest of our students' lives they will be judged on how well they present themselves. Their resume is a presentation. Their college and job applications are a presentation. Their interviews, proposals, and pitches are all presentations that will define the opportunities they will have in life.

When we tell students they have to create a power point presentation with 10 slides, and what each slide will focus on, we are basically teaching them to not stand out. How many "death by powerpoints" have you had to sit through as an adult? How many boring resumes and job applications have you seen? The world is filled with people who want to do things like everyone else does things...let's not make that mistake in teaching our students.

---

[13] http://www.sparkol.com/blog/8-classic-storytelling-techniques-for-engaging-presentations/

Give students choice in the following:

   a) The technology they use to present. Don't limit students to one presentation software. Let them use Keynote, Prezi, Google Slides, Haiku Deck...and hundreds of other presentations tools that are available to use (for free).

   b) Setting the scene for the audience. Is the room dark or light? Are you giving handouts to the audience? Is their music involved? Be creative!

   c) Interaction with the audience. Is the presentation a stand and deliver type of talk, or are the students engaging with their audience? Are they using technology to engage or other verbal or non-verbal cues to generate discussion?

   d) Follow-up resources. What kinds of questions will you audience have after the presentation? How can they get more information? In what ways can you help reinforce this learning experience?

When you walk students through the choices they have in creating the presentation, delivering the presentation, and following up on the presentation...you will open their eyes to possibilities and questions they might never have even thought about during the process.

Above all else, these three steps put the presentation into a new context. It is not another assignment that they have to complete. It has a purpose, a focus, and lots of choice built into the process. Each step gives the students more ownership of their creative work, and puts the power back in their hands of what to make and how to deliver it in the best way possible.

If stories are one of the most powerful ways to learn, let's make sure our students have the opportunity to tell lots of them, and get better each time at refining their process and craft. They'll be presenting for the rest of their lives in one way or another, and it is our job to make sure they have a chance to stand out and speak up, regardless of the content they are presenting.

Learn more about choice in story at learningbychoice.com.

CHAPTER NINE

CHOICE IN PURPOSE

In the late 1960s Walter Mischel ran a number of experiments on children at Stanford University to test self-control and delayed gratification. The "Marshmallow Test" (as it was called) asked children to stay in a room with a marshmallow on the table. The child could eat the marshmallow right away, or wait while the researcher stepped out for a few minutes, and receive two marshmallows.

As you can imagine, it was very difficult for most of the children to wait for the researcher to come back in the room and receive the second marshmallow. Only thirty percent of the children tested were able to wait the 15 minutes needed to receive the second treat.

The interesting piece of this study did not come out until years later when Mischel began to ask his daughter (who was involved in the experiment) about some of her friends who were also part of the Marshmallow Test. He began to see an informal trend: The children who had waited and delayed gratification, seemed to be more successful in certain areas of life than the children who had ate the marshmallow right away.

This led Mischel and his team to do an extensive follow-up on the participants of the Marshmallow Test study. What they found directly correlated to the hunch Mischel had while speaking to his daughter: The group of children who had waited for the second marshmallow had higher SAT scores (by over 200 points), lower Body Mass Index, more educational attainment, among other benefits.

"What we're really measuring with the marshmallows isn't will power or self-control," Mischel says. "It's much more important than that. This task forces kids to find a way to make the situation work for them. They want the second marshmallow, but how can they get it? We can't control the world, but we can control how we think about it."[14]

The lack of self-control and situational purpose is something many people (not just kids) struggle with in their lives. We all want more out of school, out of our jobs, out of our relationships, and out of life...but as the Marshmallow Test demonstrates, it takes more than wanting something to overcome a challenge.

Without Purpose the Process Will Stop

I used to think all I needed to create something that mattered was passion...I was wrong. It turns out passion might start the engine and get the creative process moving, but purpose is what takes it all the way to the destination (and beyond). Purpose allows you to wait 15 minutes (or years) for a greater reward. Passion tends to fizzle out in 30 seconds before we move onto something else.

I learned this the hard way when I started to write my first (would be) book. It was going to be titled, *The Quantified Teacher*. I wanted to quantify the teaching practice and record how much time I spent doing various teaching activities throughout the day. My ultimate hope was to expose some sort of truth that the teaching practice is

---

[14] http://www.theatlantic.com/health/archive/2014/09/what-the-marshmallow-test-really-teaches-about-self-control/380673/

much more than standing in front of the classroom, and our jobs require a great deal of creativity and flexibility. I recorded my activities, polled other teachers on what they did on a weekly basis, and looked through a lot of research on the subject...and then I stopped.

I never even published a blog post on my findings after initially polling teachers (shame on me). I lost some of that initial passion for this idea and never had enough purpose to carry it all the way to the finish line. I realized the amount of time and effort I would have to put into writing this book and it wasn't worth it. Why? Because my purpose was not strong enough, nor focused.

This wasn't the only time my passion fizzled out

Six months after shutting down our teacher lesson plan and collaboration site "Collabo", two other companies received multi-million dollar rounds with painstakingly similar ideas. What was worse is how much better they were at executing and shipping their idea than our team was...

We started "Collabo" as a place for teachers to share lesson plans and resources...but more importantly, as a space where we could collaborate together on all the ideas we were "talking about" on Twitter and social media. I was very passionate about the role collaboration plays in education, and I still am, but as a group...we never had the true purpose to leave the classroom and run with this site full-time.

I received a call from a friend a few months after we shut down "Collabo" and he said "I'm sure you heard about those two companies closing big rounds... Don't worry about it, just use it as validation that you were on to something. And that you had the timing close to perfect. Most people never make it that far. Now you can reflect on what it means to ship a product."

Learning from Failure

To be honest, I wasn't devastated. I realized "Collabo" was more of a side project to us (we all kept our real jobs as teachers) and I knew that I gave up control long ago, when we brought in a developer from the outside. The thing that hurt was trying to internally look at my own reasons and purpose for starting our company.

I don't want my work to be just another fad in education. I've been great at jumping on fads my entire life. From Pong to Pokemon, skateboarding to rollerblading, cargo sweatpants to skinny jeans, Nextel to Razor to Blackberry to iPhone...this list could go on. I'm constantly looking out for the "next new thing". I thoroughly enjoy adopting and embracing most things *new*.

As a teacher this has helped me because my classes stay innovative, and I stay up-to date on what is happening in education and around the world. As a coach this has helped me because I'm always looking for new ways to motivate and game plan. But as a *creative* this has given me a tendency to move onto the "next big thing" instead of focusing on what's important.

In the last few years I've learned to really focus on projects that I'm not only passionate about, but also have a purpose that can carry me through the difficult times in the creative process. I've gone from a passionate creator, to a purposeful creator. And it's made all the difference.

Purpose, Grit, and Finishing

This is not a new phenomenon. Leaders, politicians, businesses, and teachers have seen over time the effects a driving purpose can have on everything from winning an election to selling more of a product. Psychologists like Walter Mischel have been studying and researching this in depth since the 1960's, when he launched the

"Marshmallow Test" and found the benefits of "self-control" outweighed IQ.

In education right now, the buzz-word is "GRIT". University of Pennsylvania Professor Angela Duckworth is one of the leading researchers in the field of Grit, and her work has made waves. Duckworth analyzed a Catherine Morris Cox study of 300 recognized geniuses and found two specific qualities that she believed to be a better predictor of high achievement than anything else:

The tendency not to abandon tasks from mere changeability. _Not seeking something because of novelty. Not "looking for a change."_

The tendency not to abandon tasks in the face of obstacles. _Perseverance, tenacity, doggedness._[15]

Duckworth called the presence of these two qualities, _Grit_. She (and her colleagues) devised a short test to measure an individual's "Grit" Score. What I found fascinating about her work is how "purpose" can be a driving force behind a person's grit. A recent New York Times article summarizes her work (and findings) this way:

People who accomplished great things, [Duckworth] noticed, often combined a passion for a single mission with an unswerving dedication to achieve that mission, whatever the obstacles and however long it might take.

Passion without dedication often leads to nothing. As I mentioned above in my story, passion is not enough. When I look at what creative projects I've successfully finished and published, they come from a similar equation:

- The Best and Next in Education – I'm passionate about making digital products and wanted to work on a digital magazine, but my purpose was to "push the best educational

---

[15] http://99u.com/articles/7094/the-future-of-self-improvement-part-i-grit-is-more-important-than-talent

content" out to teachers and leaders who aren't spending time on Twitter, or reading blogs.

- The Complete Guide to 20% Time (and Genius Hour) in the Classroom - This four-part video course was something I wanted to create for a long time. It goes over the basics of how to run an inquiry-based project in your classroom, and takes it a step further by walking through the steps to make it successful.
- Inquiry and Innovation in the Classroom – I was passionate about publishing a real book but never could even create a proposal until I found a true purpose. My purpose for this book is to show teachers, parents, and administrators that inquiry-driven learning experiences foster innovative students, teachers, and schools.

And the book you are reading right now is another example of how purpose gave my idea staying power. Passion with real purpose gave me the "grit" to finish what I started in the creative process.

Adding Purpose to the Learning Process

When I ran the 20% time project in my classroom, a few things were immediately apparent to me:

1. My students had a hard time uncovering passion in the school setting.

2. I had a difficult time helping them find their passion.

3. Almost all of the successful projects had a driving purpose behind them.

Last year, as I help out other teachers who are running inquiry-based projects like 20% time and Genius Hour, I'm always asking students what their purpose is in whatever they are working on. I explain that it's also what I ask myself when I'm working on something creative. Their purpose could be to change the world, or make a video game that 1000 people play, or start a band. But as long as they truly care about that purpose, they'll have the dedication needed to keep going when the process is difficult.

How often is the only "purpose" for learning tied to grades? How often is the only "purpose" for work tied to money? What happens to learners who don't care about grades, and workers who want more purpose in their job than just a paycheck? Chances are they stall out, fail to move forward, and move on to something else.

If we want creative students, we'll have to allow them to choose a purpose for much of their learning. If we want creative teachers and leaders, we need to allow for purposes other than financial compensation. The creative process cannot be forced and it cannot be faked. It must contain purpose or it will never be realized.

A Step-by-Step Process for Giving Students Choice in their Learning Purpose

If we go back to the graphic shown in Chapter 2 of "levels of engagement" you'll remember that an engaged classroom has two specific qualities: high attention and high commitment.

High attention can come from a variety of teacher decisions and actions in the classroom. You could be putting on some type of show, be funny, tell an interesting story, or craft a unique simulation or demonstration that captures the entire class's attention. While high-attention is usually a mix of the environment and student buy-in, high commitment is intrinsic and must be connected to purpose.

The **first step** to giving students choice in their learning purpose is to actually define that purpose on their terms. Yes, there is curriculum, content, and standards you have to cover as a teacher. But at the start of a school year or new semester, give students an opportunity to define and create three types of goals.

As an aside, with elementary students you may not want to go into as much detail with the career and lifestyle goals...but I do think it is important that students see their learning as connected to "who they want to be" and "what they want to do" when they are older.

Academic Goals: These goals are directly tied to the type of learning they are doing in your class and at school in general, although they should not be limited by the particular class, subject, or grade level.

Career Goals: These goals look forward towards a career. What career do they want to have, and what does success look like in that career? Students will often change career goals and that is fine (as I've changed career goals many times already!).

Lifestyle Goals: What type of life do they want to live? This is not about money, but it could include money. Do they want to work 70 hour weeks at a high-powered job, or work 30 hours a week while traveling remotely? Many times students need to be exposed to more types of lifestyles in order to understand the thousands of options.

The **second step** is to consistently ask, "Why do you want to learn this?" Once students have defined their goals, then they have created a purpose for learning. Often the learning in the class will tie back to their academic goals, but hopefully it can ultimately tie back to their career and lifestyle goals as well.

Here's an example: A student has defined his lifestyle goal as traveling the world while working remotely 30-40 hours a week. He realizes most of the work he'll have to do is freelance contract work for individuals and companies. His career goal is to learn enough freelancing that he could end up creating his own business that can run on his own terms. He is interested in building websites and apps as a potential business. His academic goals are to take classes that will help him gain skills to build websites and apps in order to start freelancing while he is in college (if he needs to go to college). Work that he is doing in Algebra, Geometry, English, or Physics can be directly tied to all three types of goals.

The **third step** is more for the teacher, it is asking, "How is this authentic or connected to their lives and goals?" We have the ability to take dry material and make it authentic. When you've taken the time to see your students' goals on display, it would be hard not to take them into account while creating activities and assessments. You could stand in the front of the room, lecture from a power point, and drill facts and information at your class...or you could create the type of lesson, activity, or assessment that is shared in Chapters 1-8. A student's purpose can only last for so long when he/she sees that the class has little relevance to where they want to go in life. Make sure they see a connection, and engagement will follow.

The **fourth step** is creating peer accountability. The key to this step is to understand that purpose-driven students are contagious. They infect life and energy into a classroom and subject. If another student's actions are prohibiting the class from reaching their goals, then peer accountability can handle it in ways a teacher cannot. This type of classroom environment is similar to a team environment at work or in sports. Each player or team member has their own goals and responsibilities, but they must work together for the benefit of everyone involved. When someone doesn't hold up their end of the work, the team needs to hold them accountable. Have students work in groups, and make sure they have shared goals along with their personal goals. Positive peer pressure will take care of the rest!

When you've successfully taken these four steps with your class, a new type of learning will happen in (and out) of the classroom. Students will be not only be engaged, but they'll also care. They'll care about their learning, about their work, and about their place in helping the entire class move forward. The key is giving them a choice in defining their learning purpose.

Learn more about choice in purpose at learningbychoice.com.

CHAPTER TEN

WHAT TO DO WHEN STUDENTS STRUGGLE WITH CHOICE

A teacher I work with asked me, "How do we deal with those students who aren't doing anything with their time when I give them choice? I feel like I've helped and helped...but they don't seem to care at all."

Maybe you've had this same experience with a student (or group of students) while running a choice-based activity or assessment in your class. Maybe it is something that worries you about starting this type of learning project where students get to choose their learning path, and delve into their interests and passions.

While inquiry-based learning may be scary (and exciting) for many students, it can also be difficult for a teacher to manage--especially when the freedom you've given students is used to do "nothing".

Freedom Comes with Responsibility

First, let me set the context a bit. Since I ran a 20% time project in my class a few years ago teachers in my school district embraced the idea of choice-based learning. We had various teachers present to our staff on the benefits of this type of learning opportunity. And as a district we wrote "Genius Hour" into our 9th Grade Common Core Language Arts curriculum.

Students at my school will hopefully be exposed to this project for the foreseeable future (or until we revamp the curriculum completely) and I am so impressed with the 9th grade teachers' abilities to work with their students over the past two years.

Second, this question is not a new one. I'd be hard-pressed to find a teacher who has run an inquiry-based or choice-based project in their class and not dealt with some resistance from students. I had many students who "pushed back" at first…either saying they didn't have anything to work on, or who wanted to use the 20% time to do work they had for other classes.

Yet, it is a difficult position for a teacher to be in. We've given students the "freedom to learn what they want", but with that freedom comes more responsibility than some students are used to. They no longer have the "reward or punishment" of traditional learning hanging over their heads, and for some this gives them all the reason in the world to do nothing.

Don't Blame the Student

When this happened in my class my first thought was to blame the student. I couldn't believe they would take the freedom to learn what they want and turn up their nose. Luckily, I quickly snapped out of that thought-process. Blaming the student not only fails to solve this problem, but it also misses the entire point of inquiry-based learning.

I open every Genius Hour or 20% Time talk with the same three points:

> *Problem #1: Students are not allowed to learn what they want. And instead learn to play the game of school.*
>
> *Problem #2: Students graduate or leave high school without knowing what they are passionate about or having a true purpose for learning other than grades.*
>
> *Problem #3: The world is filled with many adults who hate what they do for a living. Only doing it to get by.*

When a student chooses to do nothing with their time, it is not a complete "failure". It's merely their reaction to "Problem #1". They've spent much of their schooling fighting for a grade, complaining about grades, or worrying about grades. Every paper, project, and assignment they've worked on has been crafted by a teacher (or textbook) with guidelines, steps, and usually a rubric for evaluation.

If you don't remember what it was like to be a student, let me tell you: It's exhausting.

So, when a student chooses to do nothing, resist your urge to be mad and/or upset and instead focus on getting to the root of the issue.

Choice Never Fails

I was the type of student who loved to fly under the radar. I was completely content with getting "B's" and sitting in the back of the class. I was friendly and didn't cause too much trouble, but mostly I didn't want to be bothered with school. I often wonder how I would have handled the freedom we give our students during choice-based activities.

Relationships

The three steps I've taken in the past (and try to help other teachers take) are based on my initial experience with this issue, and how it reminded me clearly of my own education experience.

Step 1: Talk with the student about life (not the project)

Have a conversation (or a few conversations) about life in general with the student who is doing nothing. It's simple, but something that all the great teachers in my life have in common is their ability to talk with me. When I've noticed a teacher caring about me the person, instead of only me the student, I've responded positively.

The structure of inquiry-driven learning allows for teachers to talk with each student individually. Many students will want your advice on their project or ask you questions about their ideas...but some will shy away from this one-on-one conversation. Use this time to get to know your students better. For the student that doesn't want to work on anything, make it a point to talk about things other than the project and school. Share some of your experiences with him/her...it will make all the difference in forming a stronger connection.

Step 2: Ask them for help

Most of the teachers in my school actually participate in inquiry-based learning by doing their own projects along-side their students. This is a great way to model the learning process, especially when we can share our *epic failures* with students. This also provides an opportunity to ask the student who isn't doing anything for help.

It can be something small and trivial, but I would ask for help with little things. I'd also ask this student to video what the class is doing. Recording the progress of certain projects, and give them a few questions to ask each student on camera. Keep them active helping you and other students...because motion creates motion.

Step 3: Find a new purpose

While passion and curiosity play a big part in my life...nothing inspires me to create and actually act than purpose. As I mentioned above, the only purpose for learning in school this student has experience with is grades.

They need to find a new purpose.

Have you ever thought about letting them make money with a choice-based project? I didn't until I tried it with one student and they went into hyper-drive! This particular student told me he couldn't wait to get out of school so he could start making some real money. I told him that I like money too...

We talked about what he would do to make money, and he told me that he makes money now designing t-shirts (bingo). He wanted to start his own brand. I asked why he didn't bring this up before and he said, "They don't let you make money in school, man."

When I told him he could use this project to make his own t-shirt designs and sell them...he almost didn't believe me. When I hooked him up with a friend of mine who had recently started his own shoe company, he knew I was serious!

The point here is simple: **You don't need to create the desire as a teacher. Instead, our job is to help students connect their existing desires to this project as a new purpose for learning.**

This is why I say that choice never fails. Even when you think you've failed as a teacher. Even when that student spends their time "doing nothing"-- you've already succeeded in giving them choice.

They may not take the choice and run with it right away. They may think this is a trick. They may not believe the freedom you've given them is actually real. But if you take the time to get to know this student you may realize that this is a first step. The next time their given choice maybe they'll handle it differently. All we can do is support our students through this process as best possible. We can't predict what type of impact it will have on their future, but believe me, it will have an impact.

NOTES & RESOURCES

Thank you for reading! I hope you enjoyed this book and took away some step-by-step strategies to bring choice into your classroom.

Each chapter in the book has a corresponding webpage with more resources and information available. You can access these resources by going to learningbychoice.com or by going to each chapter:

- Chapter 1: learningbychoice.com/chap1
- Chapter 2: learningbychoice.com/chap2
- Chapter 3: learningbychoice.com/chap3
- Chapter 4: learningbychoice.com/chap4
- Chapter 5: learningbychoice.com/chap5
- Chapter 6: learningbychoice.com/chap6
- Chapter 7: learningbychoice.com/chap7
- Chapter 8: learningbychoice.com/chap8
- Chapter 9: learningbychoice.com/chap9
- Chapter 10: learningbychoice.com/chap10

I know that differentiation and choice are big topics to cover in such a small book. Thankfully there are many other resources available. My book, *Inquiry and Innovation in the Classroom,* is a perfect book to start you along the path of bringing choice and inquiry into your classroom. I also have multiple books, resources, and studies linked on my research page here: ajjuliani.com/research.

If you have any questions or comments for me, please email me at ajjuliani@gmail.com.

If you'd like to get my free "Innovative Teaching Toolbox" for teachers and administrators, please head over to ajjuliani.com/toolbox for this free download of resources and ebooks!

.

ABOUT THE AUTHOR

A.J. Juliani is the Education and Technology Innovation Specialist for in the Upper Perkiomen School District. Previously AJ worked as a K-12 Technology Staff Developer in the Wissahickon School District where he also taught middle school and high school English. Juliani's first book, *Inquiry and Innovation in the Classroom: Using 20% Time, Genius Hour, and PBL to Drive Student Success* is currently available from Routledge Press.

A.J. was also an ISTE Faculty and Instructional Consultant with the Verizon Innovative Learning Schools project. He has been an invited keynote speaker and presenter at many education conferences and workshops. As a co-founder of Classroom Questions Podcast, the Classroom Cribs website, and Teachers Leading Teachers Conference, Juliani is working towards solving some of biggest issues in education through collaboration.

A.J. received his Master's Degree from Drexel University in "Global and International Education". He founded –Project: Global Inform – a project that gives students the power to do something about human rights violations, after being involved with the award winning Flat Classroom Project.

A.J. lives just outside of Philadelphia, PA with his wonderful wife (Katie) and three crazy kids (Kylie, Tucker, and Mason).

Learn more at ajjuliani.com or connect with him on Twitter @ajjuliani.

52920794R00065

Made in the USA
Lexington, KY
14 June 2016